Doorway to the Sacred

Transform Your Life with Mantra Prayer

OTHER BOOKS BY REV. STEPHANIE RUTT

An Ordinary Life Transformed: Lessons for Everyone from the Bhagavad Gita

The Interfaith Worship Manual: The Resource for Creating Interfaith Worship Services

Living the Prayer of Jesus: A Study of the Lord's Prayer in Aramaic

To see a complete listing of works and related products by Rev. Stephanie Rutt, please visit tolinterfaithtemple.org. You are also invited to "Like" Rev. Stephanie Rutt's author page on Facebook and follow her via Twitter at @TOLinterfaith.

Doorway to the Sacred

Transform Your Life with Mantra Prayer

Created by Rev. Stephanie Rutt, Interfaith Minister
Presiding Minister, *The Tree of Life Interfaith Temple*
Director of *The Tree of Life School for Sacred Living, LLC*

TREE OF LIFE PUBLISHING
Amherst, New Hampshire

ISBN: 978-0-9848373-2-8

Printed in the United States of America

Cover design by Amy Blanchard

The phrase "Mantra Prayer" was used by Swami Satchidananda in "The Function of Mantra Prayer" published in *Cross Currents*, June 1, 1974, Vol. 24, Issue 2–3, pp. 332–348.

Published by:
Tree of Life Publishing
Amherst, New Hampshire 03031
www.tolinterfaithtemple.org

Created by Rev. Stephanie Rutt, Interfaith Minister
Presiding Minister, *The Tree of Life Interfaith Temple*
Director, *The Tree of Life School for Sacred Living, LLC*

The phrase "Mantra Prayer" was used by Swami Satchidananda in "The Function of Mantra Prayer" published in Cross Currents, June 1, 1974, Vol. 24, Issue 2–3, pp. 332–348.

In Memory of Thomas Ashley-Farrand
Namadeva Acharya

Contents

I recognize the feeling.
Caught.
Breathless.
Remembering. Forgetting.
Some unexpected and unforeseen yearning fulfilled.
Suspended from knowing.
Free falling, yet cradled, into the sweet abyss of unknowing.

I have been here before . . . when I first heard the . . .
Gayatri mantra in Sanskrit
Kal Akal mantra in Gurmukhi
Allah Ya Jamil mantra in Arabic
Lord's Prayer in Aramaic
Psalm 23 in Hebrew.

Last sounds before sleep.
First sounds upon waking.
And, each day carving deeper and deeper.

And each time . . .
I can't remember how I was when I began and I don't know where I may land.

For, like a bell echoes on the summer's breeze, each sound calls me home
and, together, they sing to me softly, chiming in the wind . . .

A kind of lullaby known only to the Beloved.

And, I . . . I am rocked to sleep . . . even as I am waking . . .

Rev. Stephanie Rutt

The Journey to Now

A Personal Reflection of Acknowledgment

I've always loved the saying, *"Many are the ways we pray to One God."* Early in my life I heard this and believed it. Now, late in life, I *know* it. And, it has been, largely, through the practice of mantra that this blessed truth has come to so clearly inform my heart. Though I could always feel the Unseen Hand on my life, it was through mantra practice that I got *tuned* so I could more effortlessly be *played* by that Unseen Hand in ways that have so often left me silent with Grace.

Over the past twenty years, I've had the great honor to have experienced many skilled teachers from a variety of faith traditions. It has been largely through their guidance and care that I have come to *know.* I stand on their shoulders for they have provided me with the practices, knowledge and with the opportunities to enter into the sacred. I will be forever grateful.

As my opening poem expresses, there is no greater gift than the one that reaches us from *beyond our understanding.* The one that catches us and won't let go. The one that reveals us to ourselves. The one that leaves us silent. And glad. Such has been my experience with mantra. What is offered here is a brief description of my experience across faith traditions which naturally includes acknowledgment of the many wonderful teachers with whom I've been blessed to study.

The first time I heard Thomas Ashley-Farrand (Namadeva Acharya), to whom this book is dedicated, chant the long form of the great Hindu *Gayatri,* I knew there was no choice. I was captured and so I started a forty day practice. Little did I know it would be nine months before it would be done with me – for the time being. I completely understand why it is called the "Mother" of all mantras as it provides a thorough and complete tune up – up to the most harmonious of vibrations. Namadeva Acharya's teachings and stories also opened me to the depth of Hindu mythology and allegory which enhanced my many years of study of the *Bhagavad Gita.* I was grateful to be able to attend workshops with him at *The Yoga Space* in Keene, NH, and our *Tree of Life School for Sacred Living* community here was blessed to have him visit for several days the spring before his passing. He said he wanted to come help support our interfaith work and it was a visit we will all remember with joyful loving gratitude.

And, how many times have I used the beloved Buddhist mantra, *Om Mani Padme Hung*? This mantra is particularly dear to me as it captures the key essence of my work: as the jewel in the heart of the lotus, we too *blossom, not in spite of, but because of.* Though I have not been blessed to have a Buddhist teacher, Robert Jonas of the Empty Bell in Northampton, MA, has come to share his forty years of experience with Christian and Buddhist meditation and dialogue with our community and we have all been blessed. It was also through the practice of insight, or *Vipassana,* meditation, many years ago that I first had an *experience* of the One who watches. This was when I completely got that there was a difference between my mind and my soul. Profound and absolutely freeing.

And, I can still remember the very moment I first heard the Sikh mantra *Kal Akal.* Oh my, this one captured me for two and a half years, every morning, in a walking practice. My husband would later comment, much to my surprise, that it had been his watching me waltz down the driveway to *Kal Akal* every morning that had inspired him to join my *Bhagavad Gita* study group. And, inspiring, indeed, for this mantra reminds us that we are made of *Akal,* the infinite and eternal. For many years, I taught Kundalini yoga and was immersed in the Sikh mantras. I also participated in a yearlong study of Sikhism which I enjoyed very much where I was the only non-Sikh in the group! Along this path, I was blessed to have a very dear and expert teacher, Gurucharan Singh Khalsa, Ph.D., who supported both my personal development as well as the expansion of our spiritual community. There are no words sufficient to express my gratitude. Hari Kaur Khalsa also came to bless our community many times.

And then one day I was invited to go to Cambridge, MA, to experience something called the *Dances of Universal Peace.* Suddenly, all of my loves were present: mantra, movement and prayer. I can remember feeling quite certain that I must have just landed in the candy shop of life. That first night, the woman who was to become my Sufi guide, Halima Sussman, warmly welcomed me and I knew a new journey had begun. There are so many dances that stir my heart but the one that never fails to capture me completely is one called *Allah Ya Jamil* which, loosely translated, reminds us that we are the *Lover,* the *Love* and the *Beloved.* The melody was written by a father who was trying to rock his baby daughter to sleep and it is one to which I have often rocked both of my grandchildren, who live close by, to sleep. I was very blessed to study for several years under my teacher, Halima and her husband, Abraham, another wonderful teacher and musician, in a class offering Sufi esoteric studies. There I learned many wonderful *wazifa,* or sacred phrase, practices which have informed my life in countless ways. Halima and Abraham are esteemed senior teachers and mentors, Murshida and Murshid, in the Sufi Ruhaniat International. Our community has been blessed to have them visit, initially, to support our emerging dance circle and, more recently, to share their great wisdom and love of the Sufi path with our community. I will be forever grateful for all I have learned and received from them.

As a result of my connection with the Sufi Ruhaniat International, I was introduced to the Lord's Prayer in Aramaic through the work of another of the Sufi Ruhaniat International

Murshids, Neil Douglas-Klotz. This practice had such a profound influence on me that I took it on as a faithful study and practice for several years before offering my own study groups to our community and, eventually, writing my book *Living the Prayer of Jesus: A Study of the Lord's Prayer in Aramaic.* The work of Rocco A. Errico has also greatly informed my understanding. Sadly, I've not had the blessing to study in person with either of these great teachers but their gift, the study of the Prayer in Aramaic, has inexplicably altered the course of my life. In June of 2014, I will begin doctoral studies at Andover Newton Theological School with the expressed purpose to study the sound current as it is expressed through all faith traditions with a special focus on the Lord's Prayer in Aramaic. I continue to chant the Prayer daily. And, Robert Jonas, mentioned earlier, has come to share his in depth and heartfelt understanding and experience of Christian meditation and prayer practices with our community and, as a beacon of light, has left us not where we began.

It was only a year ago, though truly it feels like a lifetime, I was clearly drawn to take up Psalm 23 in Hebrew. This has become another practice that is just not possible to stop. And, of course, I had no way of predicting that I would now be actively engaged in learning Hebrew, as a precursor to learning Aramaic, and have absolutely fallen in love with the language. "Captured" is not even adequate to describe it. Chanting Psalm 23 in Hebrew continues to unlock places within me and, like the Lord's Prayer in Aramaic, I suspect it will remain a lifelong practice. Here I would like to acknowledge Rabbinic student Michael Rosenblum, who has shared his knowledge and love for Judaism with our community on several occasions, and his wife Debra, who was ordained an Interfaith Minister in the *Tree of Life Interfaith Seminary* program, Class of 2011, and who has also shared her love of Judaism, in relation to other faith traditions, with our seminary students as an assisting teacher. Both have been wonderful teachers, as well as living examples, of the teachings of Judaism and I have felt profoundly blessed to have experienced their gifts and wisdom.

And, finally, a special word of thanks to Rev. Satyabhama Ashley-Farrand, Murshida Halima Sussman and Robert A. Jonas, each of whom brought special attention to the draft of this book and, as a result, gifted this project in inumerable ways.

I became an interfaith minister because it became impossible to choose one Path. Everywhere I have landed is God. Everywhere I have felt the blessed sound current tuning me. Everywhere I have tasted the very nectar of God . . . as close as my breath . . . as dear as my heartbeat . . . as intimate as my deepest *knowing.*

Pause. Listen to the sound carried on the wind. It whispers your name. It yearns for you.

Then, wait . . . for the sound within the sound to find you.

It will set you free.

Part 1

What is Mantra Prayer?

Sing the song of celestial love, O singer!
May the divine fountain of eternal grace and joy
enter your soul.
May Brahman, the Divine One, pluck the strings of your inner soul
with his celestial fingers,
and feel his own presence within.
Bless us with a divine voice
that we may tune the harp strings of our life
to sing songs of Love to you.
Rig Veda

Imagine, just for a moment. Imagine you already have, right now, within you, all you need to create a life of *eternal grace and joy*. Imagine you already have all you need to become an instrument of a greater good. Using Mantra Prayer, you can remember this great truth and begin to *tune the harp strings* of your life to connect with your innate divinity, awaken to optimum living and create a life filled with those *songs of Love.*

And, just what does it mean when we say *tune the harp strings* of your life? Using the analogy of the harp offered in our Rig Veda quote, let's imagine together a special harp. But this particular harp we are imagining has been stored away in a basement. It has become dusty and out of tune due to neglect. Still, we know, the harp contains all the strings it needs to create an infinite possibility of melodies and to be used to its optimum potential. It just needs a good tune up. Like us.

Using Mantra Prayer we can begin to strengthen, or tune, our own strings or innate vibrations within, which have gone flat due to neglect. And, in doing so, we can begin to create a life of greater purpose and joy without. It is important to remember we are not creating anything new by imposing something from the outside. We are simply tuning, bringing forth, that which is already within us.

And, as we are returned to optimum functioning, we too, just like the harp, become instruments of the Beloved's *celestial fingers* now ready to be used for a greater purpose. We too can discover yet unsung melodies for all seasons – now, suddenly tuning us. In times of joy, we can become ecstatic instruments celebrating this amazing gift called life. And, in times of sorrow and challenge, we can become soft, pliable instruments finding tender melodies to heal deep wounds within and, in turn, become a soothing balm for all without.

Yet, whether in joy or sorrow, we find, graciously, in response to those *celestial fingers,* we are more often becoming instruments of melodies previously unknown or unforeseen. We are beginning to get it is *not we* who are doing the playing. For an instrument cannot play itself.

But first, we have to get tuned.

Getting Tuned

All know that the drop merges with the ocean
but few know that the ocean merges with the drop.
Kabir

And, how is it we get tuned? With Mantra Prayer we *combine mantra, or sound currents, with devotional intention, or prayer, to help align the soul's innate vibrations within to manifest particular outcomes without.* Essentially, we can use Mantra Prayer as our tuning fork. Let's take a closer look at how this happens.

Hindu Vedic Priest, Thomas Ashley-Farrand (Namadeva Acharya), to whom this book is dedicated, writes from the ancient Vedic teachings in *The Ancient Power of Sanskrit Mantra and Ceremony,* of a small chakra called the *Hrit Padma,* the flame of truth, the *Divine One,* the seat of the soul. It resides two finger widths below the heart chakra, the *Anahata.* One could say this is where the entire universe resides in each of us. It is the place where, in Kabir's great quote above, *the ocean merges with the drop. This* is where all celestial tuning takes place as this is where all of the inner strings, innate vibrations, reside.

So, for example, if we are in need of healing, we may choose a mantra known for its healing properties and vibration and then support our practice with a prayerful intention that may affirm something like, *I am transforming dis-ease into ease with every breath I take.* We are using Mantra Prayer as a tuning fork to tune our innate healing vibrations, or strings, gone flat with disease. Then we are affirming our healing with a prayerful intention to align our mind with positive, single-pointed thinking lest we sabotage our efforts with negative thoughts. With the knowledge that Mantra Prayer can be used to consciously tune any inner vibration we may recognize as weak or flat, we don't just have to imagine we have all we need to create a life of *eternal grace and joy.* We can truly experience it.

A medical doctor once told me that the location of the *Hrit Padma,* in her profession, is referred to as the PMI, the Point of Maximum Impulse. I just had to smile. Truth is truth whether we find it in western medical terms or in eastern esoteric teachings. Isn't it amazing to know that all the qualities, strings, vibrations in the cosmos are vibrating in us at the *Hrit Padma* and that we have the means, through Mantra Prayer, to tune ourselves, to bring ourselves back into harmony, within and without?

And, as we tune ourselves, we begin to experience our inner universe as that *drop* where the cosmic *ocean* merges with us. We begin to truly get that God does not so much live in us as we live in God and we start to experience our oneness with all that is. Energetically, we could explain it this way: each one of our *chakras*, or energy centers of our subtle body, has a corresponding energy center, or luminous sphere, called a *loka*, in the universe. Energetically, as we intone certain core sounds, called seed sounds, within mantras, our individual chakras come into harmony with the corresponding luminous spheres in the cosmos. As we chant, we are literally reconnecting, aligning and coming into greater harmony with the Source that breathed us into life. Amazing, indeed!

Now, let's look at how mantra and prayer work together in this tuning process.

Mantra: The Connection

The word *mantra* is based on the Sanskrit roots *man,* which translates 'mind', and *trai* which translates 'liberation device.' Through *japa*, or repetition, we actually retrain the mind, liberating it from its old, often unhelpful habits and conditioning. One could also say that mantra works on the unconscious parts of the mind, transforming blocked and unhelpful energies so that those very energies may be returned back into the life force to be used in more productive ways. As Einstein said, "Energy cannot be created or destroyed. It can only be changed from one form to another."

Two foremost authorities who wrote extensively and offered numerous trainings on the practice of mantra are Thomas Ashley-Farrand (Namadeva Acharya) and Sikh Yogi Bhajan who brought what he called the technology of Kundalini yoga to the west. Both expressed similar sentiments on the power of mantra to transform mental energies. Thomas Ashley Farrand (Namadeva Acharya) writes in *Healing Mantras*, "Mantra is a mental tool that can release us from our conditioned mental habits and from the bondage of any predetermined life circumstance. The journey from mantra to freedom is rewarding and wondrous; it takes you beyond the static and stasis of everyday thought into the fundamental essence and oneness of consciousness." And, Yogi Bhajan said in *The Aquarian Teacher: KRI International Kundalini Yoga Teacher Training, Level One Textbook*, "Chanting mantras, either silently or out loud, is a conscious method of controlling and directing the mind. Happiness, sorrow, joy, and regret are vibratory frequencies in the mind. Call them attitudes, or beliefs, but fundamentally, they are vibratory frequencies or thought waves. They determine the kind of program our mind plays. The scenario we choose becomes our vibration, defines how we feel and what we project to others. We can exercise our right to choose at any time."

Both of these key teachers acknowledged the transformative aspects of mantra on our mental conditioning as well as on our ability to experience an expanded level of consciousness. This is important for as we tune we begin to experience the difference between our mind and our soul and, as a result, the part of us that is of that higher consciousness. This is why in my early years of mantra training and practice, when my inquiring mind wanted to know just what a particular mantra meant, more than one teacher said to me in so many words, "It's fine to know but it really doesn't matter. Your soul will get it." Over many years of practice, I have, indeed, found this to be true. Why? As the mind gets tuned through mantra practice, the soul, the pure expression of our innate divinity at the *Hrit Padma,* naturally begins to find its full unencumbered expression in our daily experience. We just start to feel differently, a little freer, a little less of a problem to ourselves.

An analogy I am fond of using is that of the mind being like a radio. The mantra tunes the dial on the radio to a particular frequency so that the signal may come through strong and clear. Yet, the radio is not the signal. It simply allows for it. The signal is like one of those strings on that harp in the basement. As the mantra tunes the mind and body, the signal that had previously been experienced as flat or weak, can now be returned to full functioning and expression.

To experience our soul, or higher consciousness, more and more in our daily experience just means we are beginning to more fully enjoy who we truly are. We do not have to go find our divinity. We do not have to create some sense of self that we feel is good or more perfect. We are, at the *Hrit Padma,* already divine and made of goodness. No, with Mantra Prayer we can simply transform all that is standing in the way of our full realization and experience of our true self – the self that is made of a peaceful joy that *passes all understanding.* In this way, we truly become *the light of the world* as Jesus reminded us we were.

Prayer: The Affirmation

Just as mantra works on the unconscious parts of our mind, our prayerful intentions compliment and support the process by working on the conscious level of the mind. By consciously using positive, prayerful thoughts, we actively support the tuning process and avoid the, all too common, sabotaging of our practice with the old, unhelpful mind scripts and self-talk.

Becoming more and more aware of our thoughts is essential as we are manifesting each moment with our thoughts and actions, consciously and unconsciously, whether we are aware or not. And, either way we are constantly reaping what we are sowing or, from the eastern perspective, experiencing the results of our karma. With Mantra Prayer we become more aware of our moment to moment thoughts and inner dialogue particularly as we are choosing to tune our minds to a new frequency. In fact, we may not even fully realize how flat we may have become until we consciously choose to create, for example, abundance or courage. This is when it is good to remember that if we just do the practice, the mind will become attuned and the soul will get it.

We can think of prayer as simply another form of thought, or dialogue, which can support our tuning process in more helpful ways, if we re-think what we mean by prayer. Just remembering that *we live in God* fundamentally begins to reshape our more traditional thoughts about prayer.

Let's examine this further. Those of you who may be familiar with the *Bhagavad Gita* know that this is the greatest of all secrets that Krishna tells Arjuna as our warrior is being guided to his path of greatest service. Yet, Truth, being universal, is not contained within any one faith tradition. Saint Therese of Lisieux said it this way in her poem, *The Atom of Jesus-Host*, "I am the atom of Jesus . . . for I have the Host as my support."

So, how does this blessed awareness fundamentally reshape how we think about prayer? Well, for example, you may have wondered, with literally millions of people praying to God, or to Jesus, Shiva, Quan Yin, Allah, or to some other representation of divine consciousness on a regular basis, how all of those prayers could be held equally by any one entity? The mind struggles with this, of course, if we think of God, or the representative, as outside of our self. Once we remember the great secret, *that we live in God,* the fundamental shift happens.

Recognizing, just like Saint Therese or Arjuna, that *we too* are an atom in the body of Jesus, or Christ Consciousness, as *we too* live in the heart of God, we start to get that it is our job, as an atom, to tune ourselves to the body of our blessed creator, our Host. Now, we do not pray *to* but, rather, *as,* as we start to get that there is nothing *out there,* outside of this heart of God in which we live to pray to. No, the Beloved is right here, within us, breathing us, and beating our hearts. Yet, sadly, we often scurry here and there in constant search for that which is already within us, indeed, waiting for us, one could even say, in constant yearning for us.

So, let's get about the business of tuning ourselves so, like the harp in the basement, we may be returned to optimum functioning and, in doing so, become instruments for a higher purpose naturally expressing our soul's eternal joy.

Welcome home.

Part 2

Fundamentals of Creating

Basic Guidelines for Creating with Mantra Prayer

You and I and everything in the universe are part
of the infinite flow of the divine love.
When we see this,
we acknowledge that this same benevolence binds together all creation.
When we harmonize with life,
we come into accord with the divine love flowing through all.
Morihei Ueshiba

As we have discussed, manifesting, or creating, is not a choice. It is the nature of consciousness in this field of awareness in which we live. Does a rose have a choice not to become a rose? Does a puppy have the choice not to grow into a dog? Do we have a choice not to create new cells in our bodies each moment? I think not. And our emotional, mental and spiritual bodies are in constant evolution as well. Yet, through the practice of Mantra Prayer, we are able to exercise more influence on the evolution of our experience than do our plant and animal cousins. In each present moment, we are experiencing the effects of our previous thoughts, feelings and actions and, based on how we are with our present experience, are foretelling our future. So, it makes sense that we should get about the business of becoming as conscious as possible in each present moment and to continue to re-train and re-tune the mind to support our soul's journey in the most helpful way. One important way we can do this is to own and honor our experience as much as possible and, through daily Mantra Prayer practice, extract the deeper spiritual lessons and gifts inherent in all experience.

To live is such a blessing if we know *how*. Below are some general guidelines I've discovered to be most essential to the process of *conscious creating*. They are elemental to Mantra Prayer as they provide a compass for clear direction on the journey.

First Guideline

We create according to our conscious and unconscious beliefs. Mantras transform the energy of our beliefs creating new possibilities. Expect to be put through the tapa or fire.

As we have said, mantra transforms unconscious, unhelpful energies into more conscious, helpful ones. One of the more striking examples I have witnessed of the power of the unconscious mind occurred many years ago when I was participating in a certification training program in hypnosis. I have long forgotten the information presented but have never forgotten a story told by our instructor illustrating the power of unconscious beliefs on our experience. A woman had come to him having just been diagnosed with a serious illness. She had come for help expressing her desire to get well. Before hypnotizing her, he gave her some basic information and instruction such as, in response to questions, to lift one finger to convey *yes* and two fingers to convey *no*. Once he was satisfied that she was in a deep hypnotic state, he asked some simple questions to test her use of the finger responses such as, "Is your name Sally?" Then, at the critical moment, he asked, "Do you want to get well?" And, she raised two fingers.

To become more conscious is to get to know ourselves at deeper and deeper levels. In this way, as we move though the variety of life experiences, we can remain less a problem to our selves. When we take up a mantra practice, we begin to transform the old beliefs and patterns that have perpetually caused us suffering. Gratefully, these beliefs or energies, long held knotted and stagnant, can then be released and transformed to be used for a higher purpose by the healing vibration of our mantra practice. This is why Thomas Ashley-Farrand (Namadeva Acharya) called mantras energy-based sounds. He describes the process this way in *Healing Mantras,* "Mantras start a powerful vibration which corresponds to both a specific spiritual energy frequency and a state of consciousness in seed form. Over time, the mantra process begins to override all of the other smaller vibrations, which eventually become absorbed by the mantra." The more unconscious places we transform the more en*light*ened we become. We naturally become more and more transparent, relaxed and at ease regardless of surrounding circumstances.

And, this transformation happens because of *tapa,* Sanskrit for "fire" or "to burn," energies released through our Mantra Prayer practice. Just as a good physical workout burns toxins from the body and intense breathwork brings up deep emotions for release, mantra practice goes to work transforming the mental energies of our unconscious belief patterns. Yet, in the midst of such transformation, as we become more and more familiar to ourselves, we can also experience great challenge. Becoming conscious requires we recognize and own our part in the creating of our experience. Because all of us are works in progress, this can be quite humbling. But, gratefully, we soon discover that it is precisely this ownership that moves us from victimhood to freedom. Ownership cultivates a kind of personal power that sets us and everyone around us free. As Thomas Ashley-Farrand (Namadeva Acharya) reminded us in *Healing Mantras,* "The journey from mantra to freedom is a wondrous one."

Second Guideline

We may not always get what we want. We always get what we need. Every situation or outcome can teach us if we are open to receiving its gifts.

One of the cornerstones of my teaching is *we blossom, not in spite of, but because of.* Life is challenging. It can sometimes feel unfair. God can seem to have gone AWOL. And feeling alone can be unbearable. Why this? Why me? Why now? We ask. And nothing but silence may remain. This is not the time for philosophical discourse on the nature of the human experience. No, this is the time for tender, un-tethered, holding of all we are feeling and enduring. In these moments, we want to be known just where we are. Analysis can come later.

And this is also the most blessed gift we can give ourselves in our daily spiritual Mantra Prayer practice. Something quite miraculous and beautiful happens when we are able to give ourselves this gift. What is occurring can begin to be held in a kind of spaciousness so it may find room to move through us. This loving self-acceptance of simply being with ourselves in our most challenging times is not resignation. To the contrary, acceptance allows for movement and, ultimately, release and transformation.

An important aspect I discuss with spiritual mentoring students is: *It's not about the story. It's what the story is telling you.* What does this mean? Sometimes, we get bogged down in our stories and we start to identify ourselves by them. We *become* an incest survivor, a drug addict, a disadvantaged person from the wrong side of the tracks, a disabled veteran, and on and on. I would humbly offer here that, sadly, in doing so two things occur. First, we get quite comfortable in our self-imposed identity allowing it to frame every understanding. Every experience begins to be seen through its lens and, as a result, life can steadily lose dimension. Secondly, being stuck in our story, means we miss the deeper spiritual lesson the experience of our story could offer us.

Recently at a community event, I was delighted to see a student I had not seen in a few years. Staying after, she came into my office to share with me privately. She said that she'd recently been diagnosed with leukemia. When she saw the look of shock and regret on my face, she said, "Oh no, it's a good thing. It's in remission and, really, has been one of the best things that ever happened to me. Because of the diagnosis, I made some important changes that I would probably not have made otherwise." She went on to tell me all about her new life and how much happier she was. I truly sensed a kind of freedom about her.

Now, I am certain that she would not have chosen the diagnosis of leukemia but, indeed, it seemed she received it as a sign of her deep need to make some difficult changes, and being deeply religious, to also cultivate an even more intimate trust in her God.

Author Charles R. Swindoll said, "I am convinced that life is 10% what happens to me and 90% how I react to it." Can we love ourselves enough to move through our stories and ask, "What does this story, occurrence, or event have for me?"

Should we find ourselves wanting to take up a Mantra Prayer practice for healing, for example, it is important to remember that healing can occur in many different ways and on many different levels. Perhaps, as in the example above, a "healing" is waiting in a form we could never have known otherwise. And, if we are able to look beyond the story or details and ask for the deeper spiritual meaning, we can rest assured that some blessed awareness will be there for us.

Third Guideline

Be careful of just wanting to "feel good" or creating an overly excited state.

What could possibly be wrong with wanting to just feel good or excited? Absolutely nothing! Always a much more desirable state than feeling bad, mad or sad. The problem can arise when deciding to feel happy at any expense as this can end up costing us dearly when the full truth of things finally emerges to be known. Remember, as Jesus reminded us, *it is the truth that sets us free* not our self-imposed renderings of our preferred world view. The ones who keep telling themselves that their marriages are happy may not see the infidelity or divorce coming. The ones who insist their children are not capable of serious problems may not see the eating disorder until hospitalization becomes necessary. The ones who try to ignore or control excessive or compulsive behaviors may do so to devastating consequences.

The degree to which we live in denial of our truth is directly related to our inevitable experience of what I call the spiritual two-by-fours. A student of mine who had been in a 12-step program for many years once said to me, "Before I started in AA and recovery, I would have told you I was happy and I believed it. But, it took hitting rock bottom for me to really look at the truth of my life." Unfortunately, it often takes the great challenges and shocks to wake us up to what is actually already there.

The great challenge, as well as true blessing, becomes to practice seeing ourselves and others as *both* human and divine – as we all are. This requires we remember our human folly is finite and, once resolved, will return to wholeness. Our divinity, however, is always and eternally infinite. Complete unto itself. It is only in being able to hold both the human as well as the divine in ourselves and others that we may truly *see* what is occurring on a human level and then be able to *respond* from our more divine, or conscious awareness, in the most helpful ways.

And this practice really begins with our own self-acceptance. After all, what is true peace if not self-acceptance? And, self-acceptance is the embrace of all of us, *what is,* the good parts as well as our perceived not-so-good parts. I would go so far as to say that it is the very parts we perceive to be not-so-good that need our love the most. As it is only in love that what is hurting or what has been marginalized can be embraced, felt and transformed. And what is absolutely amazing is that once we begin this practice toward ourselves, we can then begin to offer it, authentically, to others. Once we stop asking ourselves to be happy or perfect or anything else other than what is simply true for us in the moment, we can more easily stop asking the same of others as well.

If peace is self-acceptance, then over excitement, while intoxicating, is like a well enjoyed addiction. While we are experiencing it, life couldn't feel better. But, inevitably, the down side follows and we are left needing the upswing again. We get trapped on the pendulum of having the desired feeling and then not. We may not realize there is a state where the pendulum rests and we can experience a kind of peace regardless of outer stimulation. The good news is as we give ourselves to our Mantra Prayer practice, we can gradually open to the experience of that which is eternal, an inner joy not hinged on outer circumstances, and we can finally stop settling for some outer stimulus we know will be fleeting.

While doing our Mantra Prayer practice, it is most helpful to concentrate on cultivating peace and resist gravitating toward any particular *emotional* outcome. For example, if we are struggling with an addiction, we may want to start a practice to cultivate inner courage and single-pointedness to help stay on track with our recovery. If we are having difficulties in a personal relationship, we may want to start a practice to cultivate open heartedness as a way of seeing our self and the other with the new eyes of a compassionate heart. Notice that in both examples, we are not asking to *feel* a certain way but, rather, to cultivate a quality within that will serve us in more helpful ways.

Fourth Guideline

Don't limit your limitless potential! Always ask for "this or something better!"

This guideline opens us up to the mystery, the unexpected, and that which is often beyond our understanding. We will be exploring this guideline in great depth in the next section, *Working with Will and Surrender*. For now, you are invited to consider the possibility that you may not know, may not even have a clue, what may be the best path to the full manifestation of what you might imagine to be a divinely inspired life. You may have an inkling, a sense, a direction in which to point, but no clear, concrete outcome. Wonderful! I say this because one of the most important things I've been blessed to witness and experience over my many years of Mantra Prayer practice is that *it is my job to follow the impulse, or direction, of my desire and then to release attachment to the outcome or to how it might come to manifestation.* In this way, the Beloved has brought me outcomes I could have never imagined given my own limited knowledge and understanding. By following the impulse and not already deciding on a specific outcome, we open ourselves to infinite possibilities. We are then able to attract an outcome that, in the beginning, may not have even been close to, much less on our radar. This is why I love to say, *I'm so glad I'm not in charge of my life!* I could never have foreseen so many of the blessings I have experienced.

For example, if we are in need of a new job, it might be best to create a Mantra Prayer practice asking to attract, not that perfect job we just discovered online, but rather the most perfect job for us at this time. Now we are allowing for the possibility of attracting an even more perfect situation waiting just beyond our awareness. And the best thing is, if that job we just found on line *is* the most perfect job, it will still find us! We can't lose!

When we are using a Mantra Prayer practice to attract a particular kind of outcome, let's remember to follow the impulse, the direction, and then to hold the possibility that anything we may already have in mind, the *this* may not, in fact, come to manifestation because the *or something better* is already in store for us. This makes our life experience come alive as we, literally, give ourselves to the mystery – to bless and inform us.

And, sometimes, that blessing may not be at all what we expected or even to our liking. In those times, we are reminded that a power greater than all of us is doing everything and that the only certainty on the spiritual journey is the realization that what we expect to happen may not. But, herein lies a kind of hidden treasure if we have eyes to see. We now are free to do what God wants *from* us instead of what we may want to do *for* us.

Fifth Guideline

Remember that the Source is limitless. Always intend that every request serve the "greatest good for all concerned."

We live in a competitive world. And one could observe that there is a limit to our resources. We compete to get into college, secure a new job, the next promotion, the affections of a potential mate, the eye of someone who could open doors for us, the most perfect home we've just found. Sometimes we can feel conflicted when we desire something that is also desired by someone else. It is very freeing to remember that, on the spiritual level, there are no limitations when it comes to being provided with all we need to be content, productive and to bring into manifestation our life's true purpose.

The reason for this may surprise you. Ultimately, it is because it is not about us anyway! Once we have tuned and prepared ourselves to be used as an instrument for some greater purpose, it becomes a grand *'why not?'* in the universe. *Why shouldn't I be provided with all I need? After all, I am here to be an instrument of a greater good. I am here to most humbly offer my life's purpose to the betterment of all.* Like the neglected harp in the basement, once we start getting attuned by those *celestial fingers,* it is best we remember that *we are enough* and, graciously, *we are nothing*.

Sometimes I like to think of the Beloved as my boss. Why wouldn't my boss give me all I need to do my job? And, along the way, why would I not also be given all the challenges I need to cultivate the inner fortitude, awareness and skill with which to meet new opportunities and to serve in an ever expanding way? Why not, indeed!

In our Mantra Prayer practice, if we should find ourselves wanting to attract a particular outcome we know is also desired by others, let's certainly ask for what we are wanting but also set the intention that the greatest good for all be served. Let's hold a deep and abiding trust that should this particular outcome not pan out for us, it simply was not our assignment. It was someone else's. Our assignment is still yet to be revealed. Let's stay open and expectant so as not to miss it!

This keeps us in a proactive stance and clear of the victimhood trap. Victimhood would proclaim, "Not fair! That promotion belonged to me!" Proactive faith proclaims, "Wow, there must be something even better in the works for me!"

Sixth Guideline

There is no one or nothing to compete against. Do not fight "against." Instead, fight "for."

Mother Teresa once said, "I will never attend an anti-war rally. If you have a peace rally, invite me." This reminds us that, energetically, we can create opposition with some other energy, within ourselves, with another person or situation, or we can go forward creating our own new energetic paths. One example of this is when we hear of someone "fighting" a disease. I would prefer to think that, instead of fighting something in myself, that the part of me that is in dis-ease most likely needs my love in order to be put at ease and to be healed. Several years ago, I was presented with a situation whereby it was suspected I could have uterine cancer. A part of my healing journey was to start sending love to my uterus 'round the clock. I asked the Beloved to transform any dis-ease in my uterus with love, to create ease and healing. It turned out that all was well. It did not feel important to me to know if I had "really" been sick or not. Instead, I choose to receive it as an opportunity to practice loving myself a little better and, also, to look a little more closely at what might have been happening in my life that may have helped to attract this experience. We don't necessarily need "proof" when our intention is always to learn, grow and to become more conscious and aware. I share this story in Part 5: Extraordinary Stories from Ordinary People Using Mantra Prayer.

The same intention could be applied to difficulties in relationship. Instead of trying to get rid of something in ourselves or in the other, or fight against another, the relationship is best served when we love ourselves and the other enough to ask for what is needed so that a deeper love may be cultivated in the relationship. When there is this mutual intention, the more difficult communications necessary for authentic healing can be better received by both parties. When no one has to be all good or all bad and when both parties assume self-responsibility for their part in creating the dynamics, both helpful and hurtful, the relationship is better able to be healed in direct response to each parties' inner work and love.

So, in our Mantra Prayer practice, let's concentrate on creating new pathways of energy *focusing on what we would like to see be manifested.* Let's fight *for* that which will support the most optimum expression of the divinely inspired life we are seeking.

Seventh Guideline

Remember there is nothing "out there." There is nothing to "go get." You're not bringing anything to you. You are simply aligning yourself to receive what's already there.

I have saved this one until last as, in many ways it brings us full circle to where we began. In addition to the realization that you already have all you need within to live a joy filled life, consider that you have also come into manifestation with a divine purpose. This notion is, indeed, echoed across faith traditions and spiritual literature. In the beloved Hindu scripture, the *Bhagavad Gita,* it is called our *svadharma.* A modern adaptation of the *Bhagavad Gita, The Legend of Bagger Vance,* calls it our *authentic swing*. The *Alchemist* calls it our *personal legend.* In Judaism, within the tradition of the *Kabbalah*, it is called our personal *kitun*. Well known medical intuitive and author Carolyn Myss calls it our *sacred contract*. Muhammad proclaimed that we were each a *hidden treasure yearning to be known.* And, I would add that, perhaps, our true life's purpose is to allow Allah, or God, to express our treasure through us. And, the late Joseph Campbell told us to follow our bliss.

Just like the harp in the basement, when we tune ourselves we become readied instruments to bring forth our divine purpose. We get that as a *drop* in the divine *ocean* we already contain all we need. And, much like a seed of a giant oak contains all that the oak may become, so do we contain in the seed of our beginnings all the potential of what we may become. This is the most extraordinary thing to realize. Because, with this awareness, we start to get that we don't have to go get something on the outside to be more of who we may be. Rather, it is our job to cultivate what is already within. Yes, just like the oak seed needs water, fertilizer and care from others, we too need our teachers, helpers and healers. But, in the end, it is important to remember that we have already been seeded with the most perfect expression of our divine purpose. No one can give that to us, though some may be able to help us awaken to its treasure.

As we are doing our Mantra Prayer practice, let's keep in mind that all requests or intentions are, ultimately, for the purpose of nurturing the inner seed yearning to blossom and express our most sacred contract for this lifetime, in service to a greater good. Let's remain content just to do our part and hold the remembrance that the full fruition of our life's purpose may not even come to full manifestation in our lifetime. There is a great story from the Tao that illustrates this:

> *A traveler through the mountains came upon an elderly gentleman who was busy planting a tiny almond tree. Knowing that almond trees take many years to mature, he commented to the man, "It seems odd that a man of your advanced age would plant such a slow-growing tree!" The old man replied, "I like to live my life based on two principles: One is that I will live forever. The other is that this is my last day."*

Working with Will and Surrender

It is our job to follow the impulse, or vision,
placed in our heart at birth . . .
And then, to release that impulse into the unseen
hand of the Beloved for manifestation.
Rev. Stephanie Rutt

Will	Surrender
Listen. Act in faith.	*Release all outcomes to the Divine.*
I am enough.	I am nothing.
I follow my heart's deepest desire.	I trust the unseen hand to manifest.
I work as if it all depends on me.	I pray as if it all depends on God.
I show up.	I offer all for the greater good.

Activating Our Will

We have been given the most precious gift and it is absolutely free. It is called *will.* And, as we discussed earlier, we are utilizing this gift, for better or worse, every single moment, with each thought, word and action we take. It is not a choice. It is a choice just how conscious we choose to be of the process. Once we begin to realize that it is our job to tune ourselves so we may more fully manifest and fulfill our divine purpose, how we use our will, or do our part, becomes of primary importance.

Let's take a closer look at *will.* Will is very closely linked to desire. Yet, in many spiritual scriptures we are told to rein in desire, primarily in relation to controlling the senses. I would offer, however, that desire is not the problem. What we choose to desire can be. For example, desiring to lead a divinely inspired life, rising every day for our Mantra Prayer practice, sitting and witnessing the whole of our experience, is the most noble of desires, though rarely the easiest path. Yet, this desire is the very one that can lead us to freedom, freedom to courageously show up to share our gifts and, ultimately, to the remembrance it's really not about us at all.

And, once we've started on this path, nothing else will quite satisfy. The desire to know more and more deeply this *truth that makes us free* expands and becomes stronger and stronger. Recalling the book *The Alchemist,* we are reminded that we go in search of our treasure, or personal legend, in part because, "You've got to find the treasure so that everything else you've learned along the way makes sense." And, so we commit to our Mantra Prayer practice, to embrace the full truth of our experience, and to tune the mind just long enough to perhaps hear, from the deep recesses of our heart at the *Hrit Padma*, the silent voice of our sweet treasure. It is the only way our deepest longing can be satisfied.

And, once an expression of our inner treasure is seeking manifestation, something happens. The ancient Hindu sage, Patanjali, perhaps said it best. "When you are inspired by some great purpose, some extraordinary project, all your thoughts break their bounds. Your mind transcends limitations, your consciousness expands in every direction and you find yourself in a new great wonderful world . . . and you discover yourself to be a greater person by far than you ever dreamed yourself to be." This is because our treasure is only the seed of our manifestation. It holds all the potential for the ultimate outcome but, gratefully, we know not what it may be.

Still, it is our job to show up and do our part. A great story that illustrates this is from *A Travelers' Gift* by Andy Andrews. It reminds us that our gift back to God, in gratitude for being loved into birth, is to fulfill the vision planted in our hearts. To illustrate this, the book extracts well known people from history and offers to the reader what their gifts might have been to all of us. One such story tells of Christopher Columbus and his journey in search of the new world.

We are invited into the story at a critical time. The journey is well underway and there has been no land in site for many weeks. The crew is running out of food and wants nothing but to turn around and head back home. A mutiny is stirring. Yet, when the fictional traveler, David Ponder, asks Columbus if there will be land, Columbus answers, "Yes, there is land . . . and it is right there. I see it as plainly as I see you. For almost twenty years I have seen it. And, tomorrow, you will see it too . . ." When David asks if such a claim is realistic, Columbus answers, "I say to you 'no', but then nothing great was ever accomplished by a realistic person! Will we find land? Yes! Yes! We will find land but that will be the least of *your* discoveries. You will find a heart for success that you did not know existed." And, David reflects to himself, *"What could I accomplish with a spirit as powerful as this?"*

Later, the angel Gabriel visits and offers the following: *"A man of faith lives in perpetual reward. Faith is to believe what one has not seen. The reward of faith is to see what one has believed."* When David reflects that he has always thought of himself as a man of reason, the angel responds, *"Reason never makes room for miracles; faith releases miracles. Reason can only be stretched so far, but faith has no limits. The only limit to your realization of tomorrow is the doubt to which you hold fast today."*

When we step up to do our part in full faith and trust, we open to infinite possibilities where, as we are told in Mark 9:23, *All things are possible to him who believes.*

Allowing Sweet Surrender

Surrender is a loaded word in our culture. But, as usual on the spiritual path where paradox is the rule, it is surrender that actually predisposes us to receiving that which is infinitely sweeter than anything we could have imagined. Surrender is where the mystery unfolds. With surrender our task is really not to *do* anything but rather to allow God to do through us as we simply *be.*

Sweet surrender with God can happen on the bus home, in the grocery store, waiting in line at the bank. Its rhythm teaches us a kind of trust that brings a growing realization that all is truly unfolding as it should – that we are placed each moment exactly where we need to be to give what we need to give and to receive what we need to receive. It is an awesome thing to realize that, in the eyes of God, all occurrences are equally important to the creation of the divine plan. As Mother Teresa once said, "Do small things with great love" because "There are no small acts. Once we give it to God it becomes infinite."

And, perhaps the most freeing, in surrender we realize that regardless of our life circumstances, we can still live a divinely inspired life. With faith and trust, we can remember in both happy as well as challenging times to Whom it is we belong.

One of my favorite examples of this is from the true story of a couple by the name of Doolittle whose presence inspired the writing of the well loved hymn *His Eye is on the Sparrow*. Here the story as told by Sylvia Martin:

> *Early in the spring of 1905 my husband and I were in Elmira, New York. We contracted a deep friendship for a couple by the name of Mr. and Mrs. Doolittle. True saints of God. Mrs. Doolittle had been bedridden for nearly 20 years. Her husband was an incurable cripple who had to propel himself to and from his business in a wheelchair. Despite their afflictions, they lived happy lives bringing inspiration and comfort to all those who knew them.*
> *One day while we were visiting with the Doolittles, my husband commented on their bright hopefulness and asked them for the secret of it. And Mrs. Doolittle replied simply,*

"His eye is on the sparrow, and I know He watches me."

In full surrender, we do not need conditions to be a certain way in order to love God. Our love truly becomes unconditional. We love because it is simply the only option. And, it sets us free.

Integrating Will and Surrender

There is a beautiful saying from the Tao. "To know when you can get no further by your own action, that is the right beginning." It all begins with a question: What do I want? Do I want to belong to the world, spending my days in service to my own desires and needs or do I want to belong to God, spending my days as an instrument of the *Celestial Fingers* in service to a greater good? Swamis in the yoga tradition often call the latter, "being *in* the world *but not of* the world." Sometimes we think we'd like to be instruments but we feel too rusty or, as the harp in the basement, too out of tune to presume to carry such grace. So, simple desire is not enough. What is required is getting tuned so the *gift that is us* may shine through.

And, in such moments of harmony, when our will and surrender are fully aligned, we become what I like to call a *living* Mantra Prayer. We *know* we are a *drop* where the full essence of the cosmic *ocean* merges. We *know* the great secret to living a divinely inspired life: *we live in the heart of God*. We *know* we have been seeded with a divine purpose and with all we need to bring it forth.

In such moments of knowing, we experience exactly what Jesus asked of us in Matthew 5:48, *Be ye perfect even as your Father in heaven is perfect. Perfect*, you say. And, why not? Perfection as an instrument of those *Celestial Fingers* has nothing to do with perfection as our ego might imagine it. In fact, it is exactly in such moments of pure attunement, with the One within whom we *live and move and have our being,* we instantly get it is not about us at all. As Krishna reminds Arjuna, we too are just here to fulfill a purpose, to play a part, to get something done, and to, along the way, fully experience that *we too* are, graciously, a spark of *the light of all lights forever beyond darkness,* birthing all creation, as the *Bhagavad Gita* reminds us.

Realizing this, our lives naturally become a kind of *living* Mantra Prayer, sparking, serving with delight some greater purpose of which we are, often, only partially aware. And, how perfectly so. Remember, it is *not* our job, after all, to focus on the destination or outcome. It *is* our job to tune our heartbeat to the One heartbeat, our breath to the One breath, our will to Divine will. In this way, we bring our light out from hiding, out from under that bushel of ours, as the great song *This Little Light of Mine* sings, to *let it shine, shine, shine.* And, the whole world becomes ablaze with our light as we step into our birthright to spark with the *light of all lights.* It is the full intention and purpose of our Mantra Prayer practice.

Tune.

Dare to invite the *celestial fingers* to bring forth a life filled with the *songs of Love.*
Dare to remember that as a *drop* in the cosmic *ocean* you are one with all that is.
Dare to claim your birthright as an atom in the body of all creation.
Dare to imagine your DNA contains a unique role to play in the vital functioning of our Host, the Host of all Hosts.
Dare to ignite your spark to shine, shine, shine!

Dare . . . and create a life of beauty far beyond your imagination . . .

Part 3

Guidelines for Creating a Spiritual Practice Using Mantra Prayer

Creating Your Spiritual Practice Crucible

"Submit to daily practice. Your loyalty to that
is a ring on the door. Keep knocking,
and the joy inside will eventually open a window
and look out to see who's there."

Bawa Muhaiyaddeen

It is fitting that the first step in creating your Mantra Prayer practice is to prepare a crucible to contain the *tapa,* or heat, necessary for the transformation to come. This is first symbolized by the outer elements, or structure, of your practice. Over time, the body itself becomes the crucible as the *tapa* of mantra practice begins to do its work.

Creating Your Special Place

I have noticed over the years as I have helped individuals to commit to spiritual practice that this initial step can sometimes bring up the first levels of resistance and challenge, particularly for those new to spiritual practice. What will my family think if I create an altar or sacred space? What might other visitors to my home think? Will they think I've gone off the deep end?!

Creating a special space for practice ultimately becomes a kind of statement of what is important to us. At a fundamental level, it is an affirmation of what we want our lives to be about. And, it is important to know that, as we make conscious shifts, others around us are affected as well. So I always recommend, if this is a new step, to talk openly with those with whom you live. Share just what you are doing and why. Ask for their support.

People are much more willing to accommodate a change if they are included in the reason and in the process. Conversely, it is often secrecy that breeds suspicion and feeds resistance.

I'd recommend choosing a relatively small area, something private that feels intimate. I've known those who've used a part of a room or have converted large closets, attics or basement spaces for their practice. Once you've chosen a place, then you can decide if you'd like to use a meditation cushion or bench or a chair. Finally, you can consider whether you would like a small table or, perhaps, just to lay out your special items on a mat before you.

Special items you might choose to use often include pictures representing a divine incarnation with whom you resonate, pictures of important spiritual teachers, prayer beads, mala or rosary, along with any variety of additional objects that hold special meaning for you. Such objects might include items from nature, pictures of family, special items you've collected or spiritual gifts you've received along the way. This is *your* space. Create it so *it may support you* on your spiritual journey! Additional items you may also want to keep close are:

shawl and blanket
iPod or CD player with headphones
book light (for dark mornings)
timer
journal
special readings
tissues
eye pillow

Optimal Time for Beginning Your Practice

The great majority of spiritual traditions recommend we practice during what is called the ambrosia hours, between 4:00am to about 6:00am. Mother Teresa and the Sisters of Charity, many Native American traditions, many Buddhist orders, Hindus and Sikhs all begin at 4:00am. Mohandas Gandhi and George Washington Carver both rose at 4:00am. George Washington Carver said in *The Man Who Talks with the Flowers: Glimpses of the Life of George Washington Carver* by Glenn Clark, "All of my life I have risen at 4:00 to go into the woods to get my orders for the day." There, he says, "Everything gives up their secrets, even the peanuts and sweet potatoes, when you love them enough." We too, give up our secrets, when we love ourselves, enough.

But, truth is, rising at 4:00am every day, while certainly not impossible, is very challenging outside the confines of monastic life. Though I sincerely committed to doing so for many years, I finally just had to admit that, because of teaching several nights a week, I needed more sleep. So, now I rise and begin as it feels right for me. I do, however, make a special effort during the long winter months to rise particularly early as I just don't think there is anything sweeter than doing my practice in complete darkness. In fact, I also keep a mala by my bedside and will often do a silent practice even before rising.

While I always recommend a morning practice, it is most important to invite the practice to flow easily with the realities of your daily life. Several years ago, one of my students moved up to the central part of the state and very much wanted to do the *Bhagavad Gita Certificate Program* via correspondence. I confess I was skeptical as one of the program requirements was to commit to a *Sadhana,* or spiritual practice, and this student had four children under the age of ten! As we talked, she shared that with a fairly new baby, mornings were out, and by evening she was just too tired. But, she was absolutely committed to going forward. So, I encouraged her to talk with her husband to see if some other time could be worked out. Together, they decided that the first hour upon his return home from work would be best as he could take responsibility for the children. For all of them, though sometimes challenging, it worked and she completed the program, something for which she was very proud.

Sometimes when I'm feeling resistant to doing my practice, I'll think of her and feel instantly inspired! It is another reminder of the question, "What do we *really* want?"

Basic Time Structures

Many faith traditions teach that it takes at least forty days to begin to bring about a change in the psyche and in life experience. So, I always recommend that a new practice be continued for at least forty, uninterrupted, days. The number "forty", of course, has biblical roots. In the Old Testament, Moses spends forty days and forty nights on the mount, Exodus 24:18, and there are references in Matthew, Mark and Luke in the New Testament to Jesus spending forty days in the wilderness. One could say that the mount or wilderness metaphorically represents the inner sanctuary held and supported by our outer, as well as inner, crucible.

Rarely, once I have committed to a forty day practice, do I stop a particular mantra practice. Even if I am feeling resistance to continuing or, for some reason, do not feel the practice is serving me as I might have hoped, I almost always try to continue for the forty days. The reason for this is simple. The mind can be quite seductive and persuasive when faced with giving up some long held pattern. It will fight for its very survival. This is why I often tell my students to tell their mind, "Thank you for sharing. Now, kindly go sit!" Without fail, particularly when I am sensing clear resistance, if I can discipline myself to persevere, I have found some important awareness waiting for me on the other side. Conversely, more often, I have started a forty day practice only to discover that the mantra is not done with me in such a short time. It is the sweetest feeling to be held fast by a mantra practice. Some practices have held me for many months before loosening their grip. Not to worry. You will know when it is time to leave a practice for, in truth, it will be done with you, at least for the time being.

In addition to the minimum forty day recommendation for a practice, different faith traditions lean toward using a specific number of mantra repetitions in spiritual practice. To keep track of the number of repetitions, prayer beads are often used. Such prayer beads are found on traditional *malas* used by many eastern faith traditions and on the Christian rosary used by Christians throughout the world. The mala used by many Hindus and Buddhists has 108 beads correlating with the major *nadis*, or astral 'nerves', of the subtle body. Muslims and Sufis, however, use a mala called a *Misbaha* or *Tasbih* with 101 beads representing the beautiful names of God in the Quran. The Christian rosary has 54 beads used to recite traditional prayers and mysteries. Depending upon the faith tradition and the sacred phrases being repeated, a varying number of repetitions may be recommended for cultivating particular intentions.

In addition to the traditional 40 days recommended for practice, Sikhs, through the practice of Kundalini yoga, recommend additional days for achieving particular results as well as time structures for practice. The additional days and time structures recommended by Shakta Kaur Khalsa in *Kundalini Yoga: Unlock Your Inner Potential Through Life-Changing Exercise* are:

90 to confirm the new pattern into consciousness
120 to integrate the new pattern into consciousness
1000 to bring complete mastery of the new pattern

And, time structures recommended:

11 minutes brings changes to the pituitary
22 minutes brings mental and emotional balance
31 minutes brings changes to the pranic body (aura)
62 minutes integrates the unconscious "shadow mind" with the outer "positive" projection

Step-by-Step Process for Creating Your Mantra Prayer Practice

"First you make the habit. Then, the habit makes you."

Yogi Bhajan

Now that you've created the crucible for your Mantra Prayer practice, you're ready to design the practice itself. Below is a model I have used and have offered many students as a starting place to begin designing a practice. Based on your experience with spiritual practice in general and whether or not you are accustomed to using practices from one or from multiple faith traditions, you may want to adapt the model to better accommodate your unique practice needs.

Step 1: State what you would like to create or condition you'd like to change.

This is a general assessment of what has brought you to create a Mantra Prayer practice. It is usually an acknowledgment of *what is* in your human journey. It is best found by following your *feelings*. Remember, your full acknowledgment is exactly what is first required to transform the existing condition. So, this is the crucial beginning. Still, remember, as Bernie Siegel used to say, "Acceptance is not resignation." In addition, it may also be an opportunity to discern just what is yours and what is not, what you have control over and what you do not, particularly in relation to others.

As most of us, at different times in our life experience, may want to cultivate healing, forgiveness, courage, focus or abundance, these are the general categories I've chosen to use as samples of intentions for practice.

- Healing: "I'd like to recover from . . ."
- Forgiveness: "I'd like to forgive myself for . . . or another [name] for . . ."
- Courage: "I'd like to feel stronger . . . be more self-assured . . ."
- Focus: "I'd like to be more focused . . . clear . . . unwavering . . ."
- Abundance: "I'd like to live in full faith and trust that all I need to support my path will naturally be provided . . ."

Step 2: Write your prayerful intention.
This is your prayer to support your mantra practice. Remember that this prayer is a conscious thought wave affirming your heart's deepest desire and thoughts are power. The whole of your experience is birthed through your inner self talk. This is where you use your will to focus your mind with clear intention. Some guidelines for helping you create conscious prayerful intentions are:

- Start with *Thank you!* Gratitude effortlessly opens the crucible within for exactly what is waiting to happen. Start with heartfelt gratitude and everything else will take care of itself.
- Always state your intention in the present tense. You are affirming for yourself what you desire, right here and now, not begging for an outside source to comply at some point in the future. Remember, you are tuning to your Source or Host.
- Focus on what you'd like to create, not get rid of.

  Example: Healing intention: Instead of, "I'd like to cure . . ." say, "Thank you for healing energy with every breath I take."

» Remember, particularly in relation to others, it is a good practice to begin with ourselves and then to extend out to others. In this way, we acknowledge our part, or participation, and set ourselves free from unhealthy ties.

Example: Forgiveness intention: Instead of, "I forgive [name] for . . ." say, "I release all feelings of hurt, anger or resentment. For my part in creating any ill will, I am sorry please forgive me. May we both be happy. May we both be free. Thank you."

This example is inspired by the beautiful Ho'oponopono Hawaiian practice for forgiveness.

» Affirm that you have the full potential to actualize that which you are seeking. Regardless of whether or not you feel it at the beginning of your practice, know that as you tune yourself, all things are possible.

Example: Courage intention: Instead of, "I'd like to get strong enough to leave my job, go back to school, start that business . . . etc.", say, "Thank you for strength and courage to speak and act my truth as necessary. I attract and receive the most perfect job/school/business opportunity to use my gifts in service to the greater good. I welcome all joys and challenges as I learn and grow."

» Think inductively, not deductively. This or something better! Remember the Beloved may have something in store for you that may not even be on your radar!

Example: Focus intention: Instead of, "I'd like the job at ABC Company" say, "Thank you for opening my awareness to receive the best job for me."

» Affirm your birthright to be fully supported in all ways by your creator. Assume and expect that you will be supplied with all you need to live joyfully and abundantly as you follow your divine path.

Example: Abundance intention: Instead of, "I'd like to receive [particular dollar amount]" say, "Thank you for supplying me with all the monetary income I presently need. I remain open and receptive as to how I may participate in attracting this abundance."

This example relates to money but remember this same intention could be altered slightly to address others areas of abundance you may be wanting.

- In circumstances where you do know exactly what you want, particularly in relation to everyday concrete items or things, like a particular car, by all means affirm it! For the more important things, such as a new job, relationship, or opportunity, always affirm the impulse, or desire, but leave the outcome inductive, or open, for the Beloved to bring you that which may not even be on your radar.
- Remember, the old Quaker saying, "When you pray, move your feet." This is an important reminder that we must do our part on and off the mat! And remember there is a different energy in striving and over-working from an energy that is steady, single-pointed and joy filled with expectation.

Step 3: Design/Sequence Your Practice

Here is a general sequence of steps for your Mantra Prayer practice.

- Begin with stating your prayerful intention.
- Yoga, Kriya, Walking Meditation, Exercise of Choice (optional)
- Inspirational Reading (optional)
- Breath Meditation – 5+ minutes
- Mantra Meditation – 108+, 101+ or 54+ repetitions
- Sit in Silence, Traditional Meditation or Centering Prayer – 10+ minutes

» End with restating your intention.

» Journal as desired

If you are able to begin with some basic yoga, or perhaps a walking meditation with which you are familiar, it is always good to begin with exercising the physical body. Then, follow with breathwork to cleanse and stabilize the emotional body. You will find some suggestions for beathwork practice in the following section along with the sample mantras. Notice I do not recommend this as optional. I feel breathwork is a vital preparation before working with a mantra. Now you are ready to begin your mantra repetition to work with your mental body to retrain the mind and transform unhelpful energies into more helpful ones.

Following your mantra *japa,* or repetition, *it is crucial* to sit in silence, traditional meditation, or in centering prayer if you are a practicing Christian. Your practice has created the conditions for you to *hear in the silence that follows* from a deeper place in your being. Up until this point, you have been using your will, doing your part, to tune yourself. Now, you are ready to receive the fruits of your practice. As Mother Teresa once said, "God speaks in the silence of the heart and we listen." Then, I always recommend ending your Mantra Prayer practice with restating your intention. It brings you full circle and to completion. Following, you may enjoy journaling in a spiritual practice journal to record the unfolding of your experience.

Over time, you will find that many daily practices are quite nice though you may feel that nothing very noteworthy is occurring. Rest assured there is a cultivation happening that you may not fully realize until some situation occurs, a kind of test, and you instantly know that your response is different from what you may have experienced in the past. This is why it is good to be tested. It is often only then that we truly know what has been cultivated within.

Then, there will often be periods of intense struggle, resistance, challenge as our humanity sits in the fires of transformation as well as periods of expanded awareness and blissful equanimity as we begin to directly experience our divinity. The moments of bliss are the gifts of grace and last for eternity. But it is to transform that which is not helpful in our humanity that has brought us to practice so it is here that we may need reinforcement. So, let's take a look at some of the more common struggles that arise in Mantra Prayer practice and then we'll examine strategies for working with, or moving through, those obstacles as they arise.

Obstacles to Spiritual Practice

"A clay pot sitting in the sun will always be a clay pot.
It has to go through the white heat of the furnace to become porcelain."
Mildred Witte Stouven

We are the clay pot. Our spiritual practice is the kiln. As we go through the white heat of the furnace, we practice surrendering all that masks our true form. It is important to remember that being our most divine self is not the hard part. The hard part is allowing all that isn't necessary to be burned away in the kiln of our compassionate heart.

It is very often quite challenging. On the human level, we may have deep wounds to cleanse for true healing. On the spiritual level, we may fear our freedom most. After all, *"What will it truly mean for me to get tuned by those Celestial Fingers?" "How will I, my life, change?"*

Still, if you are reading this book, you can bet that there is some insatiable longing of your heart that will not allow you to fritter your days away any longer. Still, with all our longing, the kiln is not an easy place to reside. We know this. So, the minute we decide to commit to a Mantra Prayer spiritual practice, all the inner obstacles show up to the party! No, they wouldn't miss this one for the world! Yet, how *lucky for us* as now we have the opportunity to acknowledge, embrace and, ultimately, transform them – all those old wounds, patterns, feelings, beliefs and behaviors that keep us from the full awareness and experience of our inner, porcelain, divinity.

And, we know that what we resist simply persists. So, we practice creating a space of humble, spacious, surrender for holding simply whatever may be arising in the moment. And, little by little we find that, in this way, as we face the dragons of our deepest fears, their power diminishes in direct response to our resolve. This is when we discover that all those inner caves we have so feared to enter truly do hold the very treasures we are seeking. For there, as we discover the true essence, the illusionary fears of our humanity, we naturally open to the true essence of our inner divinity.

Let's look at the more common obstacles identified most comprehensively by practitioners of *Vipassana*, mindfulness, meditation rooted in the Buddhist faith tradition. There are five and, in my experience, most often represent the deeper levels of resistance expressed through our individual experiences. The first and second two are often considered as pairs and the fifth follows though, in true experience, the obstacles often blend in an infinite variety of ways.

Desire and Aversion

It is the nature of the mind to run *to* what we desire or pleases us and to run *from* what is undesirable or painful. Let's look at desire first. This one we touched on earlier. It can be tricky because it is absolutely our birthright to be happy! "So, what could be so wrong with that", you ask? The problem is not with feeling good. The trouble comes when we predicate our happiness on circumstances outside of ourselves. If we're having a good day, we're happy. If we're having a bad day, we're angry or sad. However, if we understand that all forms and seasons of our emotional life serve to help us know ourselves a little better, we can begin to experience the difference between happiness hinged on outside circumstances and the happiness resting undisturbed, through all the emotional seasons, at our very center. This inner happiness is better described as a quiet peace or joy that the Bible says *passes all our understanding.*

Desire can take on an infinite number of expressions. Invariably, it kicks in to fulfill some need the ego has designated as important and then we strive to have that particular need met. Yet, I have noticed that the more I get to know the inner joy, the less striving I do. I define myself less by what I may possess or by what I may accomplish and more by my inner state of being. Some place of deep trust begins to awaken when I remember that I am truly enough in any situation regardless of what I may or may not possess or what I may or may not know. When I am tuned into the joy of my inner sanctuary, and stop relying solely on my ability to figure things out or to present myself in a certain way, I begin to dance with God. And this dance is infinitely sweeter than any personal desire or achievement I may fulfill.

It is not that we don't enjoy nice things, seek to advance ourselves in our work, engage actively in spiritual practice or serve our community. What is different is that we are, more often, guided by an inner compass and not by the arbitrary requirements set by our environment. We are not striving for external recognition. Rather, we are praying to get tuned to become good instruments of the Divine song.

Now, let's look at desire's twin, aversion. Yes, twin, because they are opposite sides of the same coin. They go together. For example, when we desire something and do not get it, what happens? If we desire a new home or the next degree, principally to gain outer recognition, then we're likely to set up what I call the *I'll be happy when* syndrome. I'll be happy when I have that new house, graduate, get that great job or promotion, find the right person, have children, lose weight and so on. If we achieve, we're happy. If we fall short, we feel less successful or incomplete. Again, it is not that we should not fully enjoy all of these things. But, there is a difference between enjoying things and needing them to help us feel complete. The truth is we're already complete – right where we are!

But, aversion, all by itself is, perhaps, the most formidable of obstacles. Just as we can see no problem with wanting to be happy, we certainly can see no good reason for venturing into our inner landscape, particularly when we're not certain of what we may find there. This is a good time to remember that the whole purpose of spiritual practice is to bring the unconscious to consciousness, to transform our dense, dark, unknown places leaving us a little lighter. This is what it means to become en*light*ened.

The more we resist our aversions, the more often we find the mind as our jailer, holding us hostage to all we fear. In the Christian allegory, *Hinds' Feet on High Places* by Hannah Hurnard, the protagonist, Much Afraid, wants nothing more than to follow the Good Shepherd to the high places. Along the way, when her fears surface in response to the appearance of her cousin, Craven Fear, who wants to capture her and take her back home, the Good Shepherd warns sternly:

> *Much Afraid, don't ever allow yourself to begin trying to picture what it will be like. Believe me, when you get to the places which you dread you will find that they are as different as possible from what you have imagined. I must warn you that I see your enemies lurking among the trees ahead and if you ever let Craven Fear begin painting a picture on the screen of your mind, you will walk in fear and trembling and agony* where no fear is.

"*. . . Where no fear is.*" This is why the forces of darkness, ignorance and fear are often referred to as illusion. Yes, it is true that we believe, feel and experience them and, yet, they are all a fabrication of our mind, not in any way related to our true, Divine, self at all. And, this is exactly why, when we have the courage to face what we might rather avert, the illusion we have so closely held simply dissipates right before our eyes.

And, so we sit, and observe the daily parade of thoughts, some happy, some sad, some good, some bad. And, along the way, we discover, again and again, that they are just that, thoughts parading across the screen of our mind.

Sleepiness and Restlessness

We live in a very fast paced society and many of us simply do not get enough sleep. So, sometimes, when we stop long enough to listen, we hear our bodies crying for more sleep. However, if sleepiness becomes a common response during our meditation practice, then it is likely that some form of "zoning out" is occurring. All of us have adapted ways to protect ourselves from painful feelings. It is how many of us survived the challenges of difficult childhoods. Yet, what might have served us well then, keeps us from the full experience of our self now.

The well known psychiatrist, Carl Jung, believed that when we have a wound, we build our whole lives around hiding and protecting that wound. Those of us who have engaged in this behavior know how very much energy it takes to construct and continuously present a persona that we hope the world will buy as us. And, if we do so long enough, we can even end up believing our own fabrication. As we come into our practice, returning to the present moment again and again, our carefully constructed persona begins to self-destruct. Thank God! But, this can feel very frightening, often more so than need be, because the mind holds a whole set of beliefs about how and what it's all going to be like when we have the courage to come into the truth. So, the challenge is to stay awake (no pun intended!) to whatever is arising in the present moment and not allow the mind to just arbitrarily paint a picture on the screen of our mind – *where no fear is.*

And, the twin of sleepiness is restlessness. As with sleepiness, restlessness often shows up in a physical manifestation. But, I have discovered that any physical restlessness I'm experiencing is directly related to my mental and emotional state. The mind will pull out all the stops as we try and harness its wayward ways. "Ok, you've decided that you're going to sit for ten minutes but I'm going to continue doing my thing. So, let's plan our day, or rehash that difficult conversation you had yesterday or, even better, let's construct some great fantasy for the future!" Yes, the mind will want to be anywhere but in the present moment! This is because the mind is part of God's changing, manifested expression residing in the context of time and space. The mind knows best the past and the future. It's much less familiar with how to come into the present moment and become the portal to our inner divinity.

And, as long as the seductive mind is doing its thing, the great reward for us is that we are saved, once again, from the deeper, less safe waters, of our inner landscape. Whew! Escaped again! And, so we stay enslaved thinking we are free.

Doubt

This one is so big, it gets to have its own category. Doubt is the mind's trump card. If all else fails, this one will do it! First let's look at what doubt is not. Doubt is not healthy discernment. Healthy discernment pays attention to inner feelings and responses, seeks to observe with a sense of focused neutrality, questions thoughtfully and disagrees respectively. Discernment clearly sees what is and what is not and enables a response that is both authentic and compassionate.

Doubt, as an obstacle to spiritual practice, tends to originate from deeply held beliefs formed as a result of our familial and environmental conditioning. Doubt is very wary of suspending such beliefs or opening to new experiences where the existing thought patterns might be challenged. Doubt often leans toward intellectualizing, over-analyzing and proving points based upon past personal observations and experiences. It looks for proof and wants to see concrete cause and effect relationships. Doubt wants to know the territory before stepping and wants to be assured of outcomes or, at the very least, be offered reasonable explanations when expected results do not materialize. Doubt makes it easy to just walk away.

Trouble is, the evolution of consciousness does not unfold to the mind's specifications. Whether you believe in reincarnation and the evolution of the soul through the law of karma or simply believe that there is a mystery that passes all our understanding, at some point it dawns that a lot is going to happen to us and around us for which there may never be any reasonable or rational explanation. However, while we may not be able to predict what occurs in our life experience, *we can always determine what we will do with what occurs.* This simple truth can steer us away from victim consciousness and from the accompanying pervasive doubt it creates and toward a more self-responsible consciousness that remembers we can choose to be alchemists, turning the most difficult experience into a treasure of learning. Alchemists tend to grow wise. Those who doubt tend to grow old.

And, as doubt holds us hostage, and paints the old familiar patterns across the screen of our mind, inevitably our commitment weakens.

And, our inner treasures, songs, wait.

Mind Pictures

Below are just a few of the more common strategies we tend to paint across the screen of our mind related to the five obstacles. I call them mind pictures.

Desire:

> "How spiritual I'm going to be when I adopt a daily practice!"
> *Well, maybe. But, along the way, we're more likely to get in touch with our deep humanity.*
> "Finally, I have some tools to create my life just as I want!"

True . . . but God may have other plans . . . can we surrender to these?

"Ooooo, I just love the buzz I get with this mantra. I must really be getting it now!"

Buzz is sweet but, sweeter still, how we treat our neighbor . . . our enemy.

"I'm going to have a really great day, feel good, now that I've meditated. Everything's just going to be much better now!"

Yes, we are often positively affected by our meditation practice. And, also, like cleaning out a deep wound, sometimes things can feel worse on the way to feeling better. But, if this is happening, the good news is that healing is on the way!

Aversion:

"If I feel anger or sadness that means I'm not spiritual."

No feeling is ever bad or wrong. In fact, allowing and honoring our deepest, most difficult, feelings is the first step to true self-acceptance and self-love. Once our deep humanity is embraced, then those more dense energies may be transformed and re-channeled in more productive ways.

"I'm afraid to feel what I feel. What if I drown in sadness or lose control?"

This is perhaps 'the' biggest illusion. What can hold us captive for an entire lifetime can begin to be struck down the instant we have the courage to turn and face it.

"No one has ever really suffered like I have. No one will truly understand."

Having been a healing practitioner for many years, I'm convinced that we each have our share of challenge and sadness. While our stories and experiences differ, we can each relate to the same deep feelings.

"Life is unfair. That's just how it is. There's nothing you can do about it."

It's our choice. We can be a victim or we can be like the lotus flower and blossom, not in spite of, but because of.

Sleepiness:

"Forget this! Let's go shopping, have a few, raid the refrigerator, surf the internet, get that report done, clean the house. I've got a million things I would rather be doing or certainly should be doing!"

We each have ways we've adapted to help us zone out from pain and difficulty. Acknowledging our particular way is the first step to transforming it.

"I don't know about this 'becoming spiritual' stuff. What will it really mean for my life?"

'Any' shift we make within ourselves causes a shift in our relationships. Yet, the ones who truly love us will want for us what we want for ourselves.

Restlessness:

"I've got to visualize a better way! Hey, all of life is just a response to our thoughts, right?"

True. But, remember, there is One who knows what we're needing and wanting even before we speak.

"You know, I've really got a great life already. I really don't need to go fishing for troubles!"

Sometimes facing our deep fears takes time. And, part of loving our self is honoring, as the passage goes, 'for everything there is a season.' Take the 'shoulds' away and seek to treat your inner child like, perhaps, the parent you never had.

"There's just too much going on today. I really don't have time for this!"

We all have all the time in the world. It's just a matter of how we choose to spend it.

Doubt:

"What if I never experience God? What if all of this is a lie?"

Do you hold a belief about what you feel God is or should be up against your experiences? If so, you've already set yourself up for failure. We do not believe when we see, but rather see when we believe. Faith and trust are our companions as the Mystery informs us.

"I doubt if a spiritual practice will really make a difference in my life. I've just got to deal with what I've been handed."

It is never so much about what we've been handed as how we chose to deal with what we've been handed. Two people having had very similar experiences may find one lost in despair and the other, also in despair, transforming the seemingly unforgivable to heal themselves and, sometimes, to even help others.

"Who says this stuff works anyway. I want proof, or at least a guarantee, before I devote my good time to this."

If we were to have 'proof', we would never get to know what it's like to step off the edge – and fly.

Strategies for Working with Obstacles

"Let nothing disturb you. Let nothing frighten you. All passes away except God and God alone is sufficient."

Saint Theresa of Avilla

A common Christian wisdom emphasizes Jesus' teaching that we must be born again to have a new realization of to Whom we belong. The early disciples and followers of Jesus experienced what has been called *the ecstatic cry* of joy – that joy that comes from a full direct, *experience* of our inner divinity. Still, the obstacles to new birth, moment to moment, are formidable as we have seen. Let's look at some strategies that might prove helpful when the mind begins to strive for specific outcomes, avert difficulties, becomes restless or dampened with slough, or sometimes, becomes filled with doubt.

Practice Radical Self-Acceptance

The first challenge is to be, fully, *with what is.* We cannot transform and release into a new awareness anything we are not willing to fully embrace. And we can rest assured that the awareness, healing and release we are seeking is just on the other side of our deep resistance. This is why Meister Eckhart said, "It is in the darkness that one finds the light. So, when we are in sorrow, this is when the light is earnest of all to us." Often when the mind is conjuring up boredom or doubt or when there is a persistent restlessness, the mental defenses or obstacles are working hard to protect us from the next level of awareness ready to surface. I have discovered that often the deeper the resistance the more profound the hidden awareness. Persevere. Tune. New songs are yearning to be sung.

It is quite an amazing process to discover that simply by being *with what is,* the ties that bind simply loosen. As we have discussed, something we may have struggled with for a very long time can simply dissolve when held open in the kiln of our compassionate heart. And, often, we are left wondering why, oh why, we held on, suffered, for so long when freedom was so close. It's okay. We first have to be willing to step off the ledge before we can discover we have wings to fly. We must have the courage to face our deepest fears in order to discover they are simply illusions our mind has adopted as truth. And, when we do, and we witness the dissipating and deep release of something we truly believed would be in us forever, we find our self resting and silent in the soft hand of God.

Sit at the Feet of Your Life to Be Taught

Polly Berrien Berends said, "Everything that happens to you is your teacher. The secret is to learn to sit at the feet of your own life and be taught by it. Everything that happens is either a blessing which is also a lesson, or a lesson which is also a blessing." Earth has been called a kind of schoolhouse for souls and this sentiment is echoed across many traditions. The notion of sitting at the feet of our life to be taught also provides a kind of distance needed to remember that we are only here to do our part, to play a role. It is one of those spiritual paradoxes that all must be felt completely in order to receive the deeper lessons and, yet, it is vitally important we remember that in the role we play, all experience, challenging as well as the delightful, will pass. As Swami Satchidananda said in *The Living Gita,* "Everything is here to test you. Do not hate the examiner. Pass the test!" So, let's work on being good students so we can soon graduate!

I think of every experience as my teacher, most especially the difficult ones. It's helpful to remember that, right when I'm in the thick of suffering, *I know something good is going to come of this.* This *good* does not necessarily refer to the emotion. Rather, the new found awareness may be *good* while, indeed, the overall experience needed to bring the awareness may be, necessarily, extremely challenging and difficult. I believe this is the role of suffering. Suffering cracks us open to allow for new light. Yet, we can choose to accept the light or hide under our bushel.

The challenge is not to avert the emotional landscape along the way but, rather, to embrace it fully. Embracing the emotions allows for a clearing, a kind of calm after the storm to occur, during which we can more clearly receive the deeper lessons of our experience.

Choose Joy!

Choosing joy is *not* practicing the power of positive thinking. This joy is not just another mind state. Rather, this joy naturally comes *through* the mind into our experience when the mind is held in equanimity. This is why the goal of meditative practice is to train the mind so that it may serve us in this way instead of enslaving us in obstacles. It's why the Buddha said, "To enjoy good health, to bring true happiness to one's family, to bring peace to all, one must discipline and control one's own mind. If a man can control his mind, he can find the way to enlightenment and all wisdom and virtue will naturally come to him."

You can choose joy when there is a remembrance that all of life is unfolding perfectly and is, in fact, all quite good, even when it may not feel that way. Cultivating this way of thinking begins to train the mind to experience the world more from a state of equanimity. We get less rattled, less often. Being willing to experience life fully and having our daily Mantra Prayer practice to support the process, helps things to move through us more easily. We let go more easily and harbor less while receiving the gifts of our life's journey. We begin to see that it is possible to extract joy, even from the difficult experiences, from the perspective of lessons learned. We no longer need life to be good to be happy. Our happiness is determined more directly by the growing state of equanimity being cultivated in our Mantra Prayer practice.

Still, struggling with the challenges in our practice and daily walk is difficult and serious business even as we are also cultivating equanimity to experience the peace beyond the daily emotional pulls. Often we only can see in hindsight what value or lesson some difficult experience might have had for us. This is beautifully expressed by the poet Rabindranath Tagore, "When the string of the violin was being tuned it felt the pain of being stretched but once it was tuned it knew why it was stretched." Hazrat Inayat Khan elaborates further saying, "So it is with the human soul. While the soul goes through pain, torture, and trouble, it thinks it would have been much better if it had gone through life without it. But once it reaches the culmination of it then, when it looks back, it begins to realize why all this was meant: It was meant to tune the soul to a certain pitch."

Radical self-acceptance enables us to sit at the feet of our life to be taught. Being taught transforms our fears and struggles into a kind of compost from which we may grow a more joyful life. And, along the way, we become a little more free of the self-imposed obstacles and become a little more our Self. We tune and find the *Celestial Fingers* creating melodies for every season of our life experience.

And, we are glad.

Part 4

Practices from Across Faith Traditions

The knower of the mysteries of sound knows
the mystery of the whole universe.
Hazrat Inayat Khan

I am extremely blessed to have been able to spend many years experiencing mantra practices from a variety of faith traditions. Included here is just a sampling of practices with which I have worked. They are offered simply as a starting place for those of you not already familiar with mantra practice. There are, of course, literally thousands of mantras and if you are already devoted to a lineage of practices from a particular faith tradition, you may or may not be drawn to incorporate any of the practices below. Use as best fits your needs!

Recall in Part 3: Guidelines for Creating a Spiritual Practice Using Mantra, I highly recommend a breath practice prior to beginning your mantra practice. Those of you who are yoga practitioners will recognize the similarity with the Eight Limbs of Yoga in that the fourth stage, breathwork, or *pranayama,* precedes the following stages of meditation. Breathwork calms, as well as strengthens, the emotional body. So, we start there.

Offered here are breath practices and mantra meditations from the following faith traditions: Hinduism, Buddhism, Sikhism, Judaism, Christianity and Sufism. It is important to note that in order to truly receive the most from any particular practice, it is very helpful to have the guidance of a teacher or guide from the faith tradition representing the practice you are undertaking. Therefore, at the end of each faith tradition, I have offered suggestions for organizations and teachers with whom I am familiar should you desire additional information, guidance and support.

In addition, you will notice that after each mantra there is a number(s). While all mantras offer innumerable benefits, I have offered my recommendation as to the primary intention(s) each mantra may help to cultivate, the same intentions used in the previous section, *Step-by-Step Process for Creating Your Mantra Prayer Practice.* These practice intentions and their numbers are: healing (1); forgiveness (2); courage (3); focus (4); and, abundance (5).

Finally, I have limited my personal reflections to the "Author's Note" section of each mantra practice presented. All other information has been derived solely from the "Source" as indicated. You are invited to listen to the mantras for pronunciation purposes at www.tolinterfaithtemple.org/Audio.html

Hinduism

Breath Practices

Three-Part-Diaphragmatic Breath

If you are not familiar with diaphragmatic breathing, you may want to first practice this breath lying on your back on the floor. If you are familiar with the breathing, you can practice sitting in a chair or on the floor.

Begin by relaxing with some soft deep breaths. Allow your exhale to be slightly longer than your inhale as you relax more deeply. Place one hand over your abdomen and the other hand over the center of your chest. Imagine in your mind's eye a picture of your lungs, how they expand at the bottom and become more narrow towards the top. Now, soften your belly as you imagine filling your lungs from the bottom up. (This softening of the belly allows for the diaphragm to drop down so the lower lungs can fill with breath.) Feel your hand over your abdomen rise as you soften your belly and fill the lower lungs with breath. Imagine continuing to fill your lungs until your other hand over your chest also rises. On the exhale, imagine releasing the breath from the top down so the hand over your chest first relaxes down first followed by the hand over your abdomen.

You will notice that the continuous movement creates a kind of "wave" of breath. This is how babies naturally breathe and how we are designed to breathe. Once you have mastered the breath while lying down, practice sitting up. As you practice, your body will naturally remember this innate flow and new levels of calm and peace will permeate your daily experience.

Author's Note: The above is a composite of many writings on the *Three-Part-Diaphragmatic Breath* I used during the years I taught yoga. This fundamental breathing practice changes how we *feel* in our bodies and, as a result, how we feel in our life.

Mantras

Om Sri Rama Jaya Rama Jaya Jaya Rama (2,5)

Om – universal creative sound or primordial sound
[The most basic mantra is *Aum,* which in Hinduism is known as the "*pranava* mantra," the source of all Mantras]
Sri – Divine Feminine
Rama – 7th Avatar of Vishnu
Jaya – victory
"Om and victory to Rama (the self within)."
This mantra is called the *Taraka* or *Liberation Mantra* and will eventually burn off all karma, which is why it is called a liberation mantra. It helps to achieve spiritual freedom by reducing and eliminating lust, anger and fear.
Repeat 108+ times.

Source: *Teacher of Mantra Instruction Manual,* p.122, by Thomas Ashley-Farrand (Namadeva Acharya)

Author's Note: *Taraka* could be loosely defined as *one that helps us cross,* cross over the cycles of birth and death. This mantra was chanted regularly by Mahatma Gandhi.

Om Shrim Maha Lakshmiyae Swaha (5)

Om – universal creative sound

Shrim – seed sound for attracting abundance
Maha – "much" abundance!
Lakshmiyae – presiding deity over the principle of abundance
Swaha – salutation/invocation at the solar plexus chakra
Lakshmi is the source for spiritual abundance, health, inner peace, financial wealth, friendship, the love of children and family. This is a powerful mantra for attracting abundance in many forms.
Repeat 108+ times.

Source: *Healing Mantras,* p.63, by Thomas Ashley-Farrand (Namadeva Acharya)

Author's Note: This is a well known mantra practice for attracting financial abundance in particular. If we offer our efforts in service to a greater good then, of course, we will be provided with all we need to manifest our divine purpose!

Om Hram Hiranya Gharbhaya Namaha (1)
Om – universal creative sound
Hram – seed sound
Hiranya Gharbhaya – golden colored one (healing gold)
Namaha – salutation/invocation
This mantra brings healing energy in the form of golden light from the sun to heal the one afflicted.
Repeat 108+ times.

Source: *Healing Mantras,* p.116, by Thomas Ashley-Farrand (Namadeva Acharya)

Author's Note: As you chant this mantra, you can visualize healing golden light coming to any place in your body you may feel the need.

Om Gam Ganapatayee Namaha (3,4)
Om – universal creative sound
Gam – seed sound for the removal of obstacles
Gunapati – another word for Ganesha
Yei – shakti activating sound
Namaha – salutation/invocation
This mantra is used to remove any kind of obstacle, even

if you don't know what the specific problem is. It is also a great unifier in that it removes obstacles through the process of unification, as in a desire and its object.

Repeat 108+ times.

Source: *Teacher of Mantra Instruction Manual*, p.209, by Thomas Ashley-Farrand (Namadeva Acharya)

Author's Note: Sometimes obstacles are there for a reason and bring their own gifts if explored deeply. I would not recommend using this mantra to just get rid of something uncomfortable but rather to remove unnecessary obstacles to a specific goal or desire.

The Chamundi Mantra: Om Eim Hrim Klim Chamundayae Vich'chae Namaha (3)

Om – universal creative sound

Eim – seed sound for Saraswati – presiding over sound, arts and sciences both material and spiritual – and helps to dispel negative energy

Hrim – seed sound for seeing through the illusions of our experience

Klim – seed sound for the principle of attraction

Chamundi – the beautiful aspect of the feminine that, nonetheless, can be utterly destructive to a wide variety of negative forces (She is the crone.)

Yae – shakti activating sound

Vich'chae – to cut through

Namaha – salutation/invocation

The Chamundi Mantra is a mantra for the feminine principle of Devi as the power of protection. This mantra is said to produce tangible power and the wisdom to use it properly. It provides proactive protection and the destruction of negative forces or entities. Prolonged use has been reported to produce feelings of self-confidence or self-esteem, especially in women.

Repeat 108+ times.

Source: *Teacher of Mantra Instruction Manual,* p.190, by Thomas Ashley-Farrand (Namadeva Acharya)

Author's Note: This mantra has a great cadence making it very easy to learn, maintain and enjoy in practice.

The Gayatri Mantra – Known as the "Mother" of all Mantras (1,2,3,4,5)

There are two forms of this mantra, the long and the short form. The short form is practiced by the vast majority of those who chant this mantra. I will give you both forms.

Long Form:	Short Form:
Om Bhu Om Bhuvaha Om Swaha	*Om Bhur Bhuvaha Swaha*
Om Maha Om Janaha Om Tapaha Om Satyam	
Om Tat Savitur Varenyam	*Om Tat Savitur Varenyam*
Bhargo Devasya Dhimahi	*Bhargo Devasya Dhimahi*
Dhiyo Yonaha Prachodayat	*Dhiyo Yonaha Prachodayat*

Om Bhu – earth plane (first chakra)
Om Bhuvaha – atmospheric plane (second chakra)
Om Swaha – solar region (third chakra)
Om Maha – first spiritual region beyond the sun; heart vibration (fourth chakra)
Om Janaha – second spiritual region beyond the sun; throat vibration – power of the divine spiritual word (fifth chakra)
Om Tapaha – third spiritual region beyond the sun; sphere of the progenitors (sixth chakra) – represents the highest realm of spiritual understanding one can attain while still identified with individual existence
Om Satyam – the abode of supreme Truth; absorption into the Supreme (seventh chakra)
Om Tat Savitur Varenyam – the realm of Truth that is beyond human comprehension
Bhargo Devasya Dhimahi – in that place where all the celestials of all the spheres have received enlightenment
Dhiyo Yonaha Prachodayat – kindly enlighten our intellect
Repeat 108+ times.

Source: *Teacher of Mantra Instruction Manual,* p.293, by Thomas Ashley-Farrand (Namadeva Acharya)

> Author's Note: The *Gayatri* is a complete practice because it aligns the individual chakras of the subtle body with the corresponding luminous spheres of the cosmos. Through the sound vibration, we connect with our Creator at the Crown Chakra illuminating the Enlightened Mind, a concept much greater than what we regularly think of as mind.

*A good resource for additional information, workshops and teachers is SanskritMantra.com and Saraswati Publications, LLC. Margalo, Satyabhama, Ashley-Farrand, widow of Thomas Ashley-Farrand (Namadeva Acharya), continues to carry on the work through her own gifted teaching.

Buddhism

Breath Practices

Traditional Practice of Watching the Breath

Begin by selecting a quiet time and a place for your practice. Sit in a comfortable position with your spine erect yet relaxed. Allow your eyes to gently close and just begin to notice your breathing. Notice the rise and fall of your chest. Just notice. Invite yourself to use this simple watching of your breath to bring you into a spacious presence with your body and with the present moment. Begin to notice the sensations in your body. Again, just notice. Then notice what feelings and thoughts might be arising.

As sensations, feelings and thoughts become present, invite yourself to put them onto a boxcar or on a cloud and just imagine them moving past and away. Then, return to simply watching the breath moving in and out of your body. This is your life-breath, your connection to your Creator. It is how we know we live in a body and, when the breath ceases, it is how we know we have left our bodies. In between, we could say *we are breathed.* Allow yourself to fall into the rhythm of this sacred life-force, your breath, this moment.

And, each time some sensation, feeling or thought arises and carries you away from this simple watching of your breath, place each onto the boxcar or cloud, and just return again. And again. And again. The mind loves the past and future but doesn't have a lot of experience being in the present moment. It needs some training. But, as well known Buddhist practitioner Jack Kornfield reminds us, it is best to be with this process much like we would be with training a puppy. We don't need to beat or shame the puppy. We simply need to bring it back to the paper. Let's practice having a similar patience and compassion with ourselves.

You will notice that each sitting brings new awareness. Sometimes you'll be able to return to the breath easily. Other times, it may be sensations, feelings or thoughts that dominate. No matter. It's all good practice for it is just how life is off the mat. Return again and again. And, over time, you will find yourself less caught by the comings and goings as you walk through your daily life.

If you are beginner, I'd recommend starting with ten minutes and gradually build up to thirty minutes. At first, it may not appear that any benefit is arising from your practice. Trust that you are, indeed, cultivating a new way of being and that, in time, you'll begin to simply experience this new way of being *becoming you.*

Author's Note: The above is a composite from writings I've used to teach meditation over the years. I start here as nothing is needed but what is already available, our breath. It is so simple, yet not always easy. It *is,* graciously, truly our connection to the *One* who breaths us.

Mantras

The Practice of Metta or Loving Kindness (1,2,5)

The practice of *metta* or *loving kindness* is an ancient practice that evokes feelings of loving kindness toward our self and others. Know that cultivating such kindness is a process that can, in the beginning, bring up the opposite feelings. You may feel you are being disingenuous or mechanical. If this happens, know that you are actually being provided with a wonderful opportunity to *practice* extending such loving kindness to yourself and to know, that in its own time, even as you face your own resistance, loving-kindness will develop.

To begin the practice, sit in a relaxed and comfortable fashion. You may want to spend a little time with the *Traditional Practice of Watching the Breath* above to help center yourself. When you feel ready, begin to recite inwardly the following phrases to yourself. We begin with ourselves as we know it is difficult to truly love others without loving ourselves first.

> *May I be filled with loving-kindness.*
> *May I be well.*
> *May I be peaceful and at ease.*
> *May I be happy.*

Repeat the phrases again and again, letting the words fill your being. Practice every day for at least a few weeks until you sense loving-kindness for yourself growing. The importance of cultivating this inner sense of self-love, kindness and well being cannot be underestimated. It is the foundation of all further practice we extend to others. It's like we fill ourselves up first so we can then have a deep inner well from which to draw. We also discover that, as we begin to expand self-acceptance and compassion to *all* parts of our self, we can, more easily, offer such compassion to others as well.

When you feel ready, in the same meditation period, choose to extend this blessing to someone you care for. Picture them in your mind's eye and recite the blessing to them.

Over time, continue to extend out the blessing of *metta* to others: family members, friends, neighbors, others you may routinely see in your daily activities, all people everywhere. Then, you can practice sending *metta* to someone with whom you have had, or are having, difficulty. This is an especially beautiful practice that can also bring challenges. But, I have found, the greater the challenge, the more freedom awaits.

This is a wonderful practice that you can also take off your mat and into your life. Imagine silently sending *metta* to the one checking out your groceries, the postal clerk standing behind the counter, the one handing you your food going through the drive-through. What happens, of course, is that this practice of extending *metta* to all beings changes us. We don't ask anymore that others or the world be different. Instead, we ask that we be different and, so, our world becomes different.

Author's Note: The above is a composite from writings I've used to teach *metta* over the years. I find it the most profound practice not only for cultivating healthy self-love but also for practicing *seeing with new eyes,* experiencing and extending forgiveness, and for releasing those ties that bind.

Suggested Musical Accompaniment: *The Chant of Metta* by Imee Ooi

Om Mani Padme Hung (1,2,5)

Om – universal creative sound

Mani – jewel – the *compassion* in the heart for all beings

Padme – lotus flower – the *wisdom* that draws up through itself the muck from which it grows – all experience is skillfully used for the transformation of consciousness

Hung – (Tibetan pronunciation) throat chakra

Repeat 108+ times.

Source: Multiple – This is, perhaps, the most well known mantra chanted in Buddhism.

Author's Note: This mantra represents a core teaching in my work and writings: *Like the lotus, we blossom, not in spite of, but because of.* This mantra and teaching sets us free from any sense of victimhood and opens us to the gifts of all experience.

Gatae Gatae Paragatae Parasamgatae Bodhi Svaha (1,2,3,4,5)

Gatae – going

Paragatae – going further

Parasamgatae – gone

Bodhi Svaha – to full enlightenment

This mantra is the final part of the *Heart Sutra,* thought by many to be the most powerful of Buddhist mantra practices. A central Buddhist scripture on heart awakening and obtaining enlightenment, the *Heart Sutra* teaches, "form is emptiness, and emptiness is form,"pointing to the root of all suffering – attachment to the illusion of life's permanence. Through dedicated spiritual practice, the attachments of the mind can be realized and released but then there is still one final step to the full embodiment of Buddhahood – action. When you attain unexcelled perfect enlightenment, you must attain the *function* of this enlightenment in the world. This is how we go, and continue going further, together, toward full enlightenment.

Repeat 108+ times.

Source: *The Heart Sutra Commentary* by Zen Master Seung Sahn, July 4, 2011 posting by Al Jigong Billings at www.openbuddha.com

Author's Note: This is a beautiful practice that reminds us that we must walk the walk as our *function* in the world. We must live and make manifest, through our actions, our enlightenment in order to become the full embodiment of the Buddha.

Om Tarae Tuttarae Turae Svaha (3,5)

Om – universal creative sound

Turae – represents salvation from mundane dangers and suffering

Tuttarae – represents deliverance into the spiritual path conceived in terms of individual salvation which leads to

individual liberation from suffering
Turae – represents the culmination of the spiritual path in terms of deliverance into the altruistic path of universal salvation – the Bodhisattva path. In the Bodhisattva path we aspire toward personal enlightenment, but we also connect compassionately with the sufferings of others, and strive to liberate them at the same time as we seek enlightenment for ourselves.
Svaha – salutation

Source: Wildmind Buddhist Meditation, www.wildmind.org

Additional Source: *Foundation Dances and Walks: Dances of Universal Peace Manual*: Here it is expressed that Tara is so highly regarded that she is said to be the Mother of all Buddhas. She is known to the Tibetans as The Faithful One and The Fierce Protectoress.

Author's Note: This practice reminds us that we *go* together. We have been given to one another. We belong to one another. Our individual enlightenment both affects and supports the enlightenment of all.

*Good resources for information, retreats and teachers are the Insight Meditation Society in Barre, Massachusetts and Robert A. Jonas of the Empty Bell in Northampton, Massachusetts.

Sikhism

Breath Practices

Calm Heart Meditation

Sit in easy pose.

Place your left hand over your heart with fingers pointing straight across your chest.

Bend your right arm as if you were going to take an oath.

Place your fingers in *Gian Mudra* – tips of index finger and thumb touching with remaining fingers pointing upward.

Relax both elbows.

Close your eyes or look straight forward.

Inhale through your nose and suspend gently as long as comfortable.

Exhale through your nose and hold the breath out as long as comfortable.

This meditation creates a still point for the *prana* at the heart center.

Practice 3-11 minutes.

Source: *Kundalini Yoga: Unlock Your Inner Potential Through Life-Changing Exercise,* p.169, by Shakta Kaur Khalsa

Author's Note: If you cannot do at least three full repetitions without having to take a normal breath, you are probably suspending and/or holding the breath out too long. The breath is to be *relaxed and calming.* I enjoy doing this practice to the beautiful hymn *Peace is Flowing Like a River.* It is an easy and very effective breath practice for beginners as well as for those more experienced.

Sitali Breath

Sit in a comfortable meditative posture with the spine straight.

Curl the sides of the tongue upward and protrude it slightly past the lips.

Inhale deeply and smoothly through the tongue and mouth.

Then, close the mouth and exhale through the nose.

Continue for as long as 5 minutes at a time.

To end, inhale and suspend the breath gently. Exhale and relax.

Sitali Breath is a cooling breath good for lowering fever and cooling off anger. It rejuvenates and detoxifies when practiced regularly. Often the tongue tastes bitter at first. This is a sign of detoxification. As you continue the practice, the taste of the tongue will eventually become sweet.

Source: *Kundalini Yoga: Unlock Your Inner Potential Through Life-Changing Exercise,* p.26, by Shakta Kaur Khalsa.

Author's Note: It is thought to be genetic as to whether or not you are able to curl your tongue upward on both sides. If you're not able to do so, simply extend the tongue out as you are able. The same benefits await. This is a great breath for cleansing and rejuvenating on all levels.

Mantras

Note: Because the Sikh mantras are often put to music, there are many quite beautiful musical versions for each of the mantras below. I will recommend only the versions with which I have had the most experience. No overall preference is intended.

Ek Ong Kar Sat Nam Siri Wahe Guru (1,2,3,4,5)

Ek Ong Kar – the One Universal Infinity

Sat Nam – the essence of Truth

Siri Wahe – great and beyond all comprehension

Guru – inner teacher

This eight part mantra corresponds to the body's eight energy centers, seven chakras plus the aura. These eight words are considered the "code" letters or the phone number of the direct line to connect you with your Creator.

Source: *The Aquarian Teacher: International Kundalini Yoga Teacher Training, Level One Textbook,* p.84, by Yogi Bhajan

Author's Note: This is a complete practice one might call the Sikh *Gayatri*. The version I would recommend for practice does not come with a musical accompaniment.

Sikh: *The Miracle Mantra* (1,5)

Guru Guru	Inner personal wisdom
Wahe	Expanding that personal wisdom into the experience of the Infinite
Guru Guru	Same personal wisdom
Ram	Infinite manifesting power
Das	Coming into your life as service

Special instructions for chanting:
Chant 5 repetitions on one breath.
1st repetition – begins with *Guru Guru*
2nd – 4th repetitions – begin with *Guru Guru Guru*
Additional *Guru* repeated only at the end of the 5th repetition

This mantra is known as the *miracle mantra* as it was the fourth Sikh Guru, Ram Das, who first came to Yogi Bhajan when he was ten years old and performed a miracle of healing. According to Gurucharan Singh Khalsa, repeating this mantra 5 times connects us with the 5 elements of manifestation and takes us in a circular fashion from the personal to the infinite and back to the personal again. Chanting it allows us to clear away all the clouds to more fully realize prosperity and the fulfillment of our purpose in this lifetime. It provides the connections, attracts the situations and brings the challenges we need to grow into our full radiance.

Repeat 108+ times.

Source: Gurucharan Singh Khalsa, Ph.D., and *The Aquarian Teacher:*

International Kundalini Yoga Teacher Training, Level One Textbook, p.84, by Yogi Bhajan

Author's Note: Practice of this mantra does, in fact, open us to the miracle of life in each moment and the infinite possibilities born of faith. Because it also incorporates a powerful breath practice, it truly does "clear away all the clouds" enabling us to more fully realize true fulfillment and joy.

Suggested Musical Accompaniment: *The Miracle Mantra of Guru Ram Das* as Taught by Yogi Bhajan: A Learning Tool from Gurucharan Singh Khalsa and Gurusangat Singh

Ra Ma Da Sa – Sa Say So Hung (1)

Ra – sun
Ma – moon
Da – earth
Sa – impersonal infinity
Sa Say – totality of infinity
So Hung – "I am Thou"

This is a mantra well known for its healing properties. These eight sounds stimulate the kundalini flow in the central channel of the spine for healing.

Practice 11 – 31 minutes.

Source: *The Aquarian Teacher: International Kundalini Yoga Teacher Training, Level One Textbook,* p. 86, by Yogi Bhajan

Author's Note: This is one of the most powerful healing practices I have been blessed to witness.

Suggested Musical Accompaniment: *Miracles & Healing* by Hari Bhajan Kaur and Livtar Singh

Kal Akal (3)

Kal – death
Akal – no death
Siri Kal – great death
Maha Akal – no great death
Akal Moorat – deathlessness

This is a protective mantra and, according to Yogi Bhajan, "wraps around animosity and seals it closed. It can even remove the very shadow of death."

Source: *The Aquarian Teacher: International Kundalini Yoga Teacher Training, Level One Textbook,* p.85, by Yogi Bhajan

Author's Note: This is a mantra that is capable of capturing your heart completely. There is no doubt it dispels all negativity and leaves one in complete bliss.

Suggested Musical Accompaniment: *Kal Akal* by Guru Shabad Singh Khalsa

Sa Ta Na Ma (4)

Sa – universe, totality
Ta – life, creation
Ma – rebirth, regeneration

Sa Ta Na Ma is referred to as the Kirtan Kriya. Kirtan means "divine song." This mantra clears the mind of subconscious garbage.

Practice 11 – 31 minutes.

Source: *Kundalini Yoga: Unlock Your Inner Potential Through Life-Changing Exercise,* pp.160-161, by Shakta Kaur Khalsa

Author's Note: I have found this mantra helps to stay focused on the unchanging "truth" beyond the changes inherent in rebirth and regeneration. This can be particularly helpful when we are going through a difficult or challenging transition. The musical version I am recommending is wonderful to do with a partner, or alone can be used in a call-response method.

Suggested Musical Accompaniment: *Tantric Sa Ta Na Ma* by Simran Kaur & GuruPrem Singh Khalsa & WaheGuru Kaur Khalsa

Gobinday Mukanday (3)

Gobinday – sustaining
Mukanday – liberating
Udaaray – enlightening
Apaaray – infinite
Hareeung – destroying
Kareeung – creating
Nirnaamay – nameless
Akaamay – desireless

Chanting this mantra can eliminate karmic blocks or errors of the past. It balances the hemispheres of the brain, bringing compassion and patience.
Practice 11 – 31 minutes.

Source: *The Aquarian Teacher: International Kundalini Yoga Teacher Training, Level One Textbook,* p.84, by Yogi Bhajan

Author's Note: This mantra is well known for its ability to cultivate courage, strength and power. The musical accompaniment I'm recommending is one easily learned as it is sung in a call-response method.

Suggested Musical Accompaniment: *Gobinday Mukanday* by Snatam Kaur Khalsa

*Good resources for information are the Kundalini Research Institute in Santa Cruz, New Mexico and Gurucharan Singh Khalsa, Ph.D. of Khalsa Consultants.

Judaism

Breath Practice

Breathing Chedvah: Breathing Joy

Chedvah means joy. This joy has been described as the sharp, first initial experience of joy. Breathing *chedvah* means to breathe this joy into our souls and bodies. This happens in a repeating cycle of inhaling, holding, exhaling and resting.

Inhale: 1-8 counts

Inhaling means to aspire.

Hold: 4 counts

Holding brings the super conscious experience into the beginning of consciousness.

Exhale: 6 counts

Exhaling brings the consciousness into the body.

Rest: 5 counts

Resting, also known as the Mother Principle, means consciousness has reached its place, destination and resonates there.

The cycle of 8-4-6-5 corresponds to the Hebrew script numerical values spelling of *chedvah*.

Source: Gal Einai Institute; Rabbi Harav Yitzchak Ginsburgh; www.inner.org

Author's Note: What is offered here is the basic breathing practice. You are invited to visit www.inner.org for much more information on this important breath practice. You will find this breath simple to practice and that it opens us to the fullness of joy within, the joy of eternal *devotion* resting in the depths beyond all temporary *emotional* joy.

Mantras

Shema Yisrael Adonai Eloheynu Adonai Echad (1,2,3,4,5)

Shema – listen with every fiber of your being
Yisrael – all who wrestle with God
Adonai – the Lord
Eloheynu – our God
Echad – is One

This well loved Jewish chant is from Deuteronomy 6:4 and is arguably the most cherished phrase in the entire Hebrew Bible. It contains two important affirmations: that *Adonai* is *our* God, not simply remote and abstract; and, that *Adonai* is One. The words form the beginning of *The Shema,* the central prayer in the Jewish prayerbook, the *Siddur*. It is often the first section of Scripture that a Jewish child learns and many Jews recite *The Shema* twice daily, once in the morning and once in the evening.

Repeat as desired.

Source: *Siddur Eit Ratzon,* p.51, by Joseph G. Rosenstein

Author's Note: Chanting this mantra invites us to walk in the footsteps of Moses. Here we find humanity and humility as well as profound faith and trust.

Ahava Raba Ahavtanu (5)

Ahava Raba – [with an] abundant or great love
Ahavtanu – you have loved us

This is the last blessing preceding *The Shema* offered above and speaks of God as the One who loves the Jewish people. The full prayer describes three ways in which this love is manifested – through compassion, guidance and presence.

Repeat as desired.

Source: *Siddur Eit Ratzon,* p.49, by Joseph G. Rosenstein

Author's Note: This mantra reminds us of how great and magnificent is God's Love. We don't have to strive to be worthy of this Love. All we need do is simply collapse into the arms of the Beloved.

Repeat 108+ times.
Suggested musical accompaniment: *Kabbalah Kirtan* CD by Yofiyah

Kadosh Kadosh Kadosh Adonai Elohim Tz' Va' Ot (1,5)

Kadosh – holy
Adonai – our Lord
Elohim – our God
Tz' Va' Ot – Lord of Hosts

This mantra is found in the third part of *The Amidah,* The Standing Prayer, which is the core prayer of every service. It is built around three verses. In Isaiah's vision (6:3), the angels proclaim God's holiness and declare that God's presence fills the world, themes echoed in Ezekiel's vision (3:12). This declaration of God's spiritual presence, of God's holiness, is followed by Psalms 146:10, a declaration of God's material presence, of God's rulership.

Source: *Siddur Eit Ratzon,* p.61, by Joseph G. Rosenstein

Author's Note: Chanting this mantra elicits a sweet devotion opening the heart to engage directly with the holiness within.

Suggested Musical Accompaniment: *Kadosh* by Paul Wilber

Adonai Roee Lo Echsar (4,5)

Adonai – the Lord
Roee – my Shepherd
Lo – not
Echsar – will I lack

Repeat 54 – 108 times.

Source: Shalom Scripture Studies, Inc.; www.shalom-peace.com/Psalm23.html
The Holy Scriptures, Hebrew and English
The Society for Distributing Hebrew Scriptures
The Interlinear Bible, Hendrickson Publishers

Author's Note: It has been very interesting to notice that the Hebrew translation is not "The Lord is my Shepherd. I shall not want." Rather, the second line translates "not will I lack." This is a beautiful reminder that we are, indeed, *already full.* We may still desire and enjoy many things but not from a sense of lacking.

A Psalm of David: Psalm 23 (1,2,3,4,5)

Translation and transliteration of the Hebrew: Reading from right to left:

ECHSAR	LO	ROEE	ADONAI	L'DAVID	MIZMOR
ek sar	*low*	*rowee*	*Ah doh n eye*	*La'Day veed*	*Mees more*
will I lack	not	my shepherd	The Lord	of David	A Psalm

The Lord is my shepherd; I shall not want.

YARBITZEINI	DESHE	BINOT
yar beet say knee	*dea shea*	*bean ote*
He makes me lie down	tender grass	in pastures

He makes me lie down in green pastures:

Y'NAHALEINI	MENUCHOT	AL-MEI
ya nah hah lay knee	*men oh hote*	*all-may*
He leadeth me	the still	beside waters

he leads me beside the still waters.

V'MAGLEI	YANCHEINI	Y'SHOVEIV	NAFSHI
vah mah ah glaa	*yahn hi knee*	*ye show veil*	*nauf she*
in the paths	He guides me	He restoreth	my soul

He restores my soul: he leads me in the paths

SH'MO	L'MAN	TZEDEK
sh' moe	*lay'mah aun*	*zaa dick*
his name's	for sake	righteousness

of righteousness for his name's sake.

TZALMAVET	B'GEL	KI-EILEICH	GAM
zaul mah vet	*be'gates*	*key ee let*	*gaum*
the shadow of death	in the valley	am walking	When

Yea, though I walk through the valley of the shadow of death,

EMADI	KI-ATA	RO	EIRA –	LO
ee mah dee	*kee-ah tah*	*rah*	*era –*	*low*
with me	you are	for evil	will I fear –	no

I will fear no evil for thou art with me;

Y'NACHAMUNI	HEMA	U'MISHANTECHA	SHIVTECHA
ya' nah who moe nee	*heamah*	*u' me shaun tecka*	*sheev tecka*
comfort me	they	and your staff	your rod

thy rod and thy staff they comfort me.

TZOR'RAI	NEGED	SHULCHAN	L'FANAI	TAAROCKH
zor row eye	*neh get*	*shul haun*	*lea'fana*	*tah ah roak*
mine enemies	before	table	before me	You prepare

Thou preparest a table before me in the presence of mine enemies:

R'VAYA	KOSI	ROSHI	V'SHEMEN	DISHANTA
rev'vah ya	*kos ee*	*row she*	*vah'shea men*	*dee shaunta*
runs over	my cup	my head	with oil	you anointed

thou anointest my head with oil; my cup runneth over.

YIRD'FUNI	VA'CHESED	TOV	ACH
yard'funi	*vah eck said*	*tow*	*ack*
shall follow me	and mercy	goodness	Surely

Surely goodness and mercy shall follow me

V'SHAVTI	CHAYYAI	KOL-Y'MEI
vay'shauv tee	*hi yigh*	*koal-ee' ya may*
and I shall dwell	my life	the days of all

all the days of my life and I shall dwell

YAMIN	L'ORECH	ADONAI	-	B'BEIT
yah mean	*lay'oh reck*	*Ah doe n eye*	-	*bee bet*
days	for the length of	the Lord	-	in the house

in the house of the Lord forever.
Amen

Source: Both the translation from Hebrew as well as the presentation of the Psalm is used here with permission from: Shalom Scripture Studies, Inc.www.shalom-peace.com/Psalm23.html (The Holy Scriptures, Hebrew and English, The Society for Distributing Hebrew Scriptures, The Interlinear Bible, Hendrickson Publishers).

The English transliteration is this author's added creation.

Author's Note: Though a lengthy practice, I cannot recommend it highly enough.

*Good resources for information and teachers are Hebrew College in Newton Centre, Massachusetts and Shalom Scripture Studies, Inc.

Christianity

Breath Practice

Abba: I Belong to You

From Romans 8:15, *For you did not receive a spirit that makes you a slave again to fear, but you received the Spirit of sonship. And by him we cry, "Abba, Father."* This breath practice was originated by Brennan Manning who invited us to simply breathe in *Abba* and breathe out *I belong to you*. Manning said, "Define yourself radically as one beloved by God. This is the true self. Every other identity is illusion."

Source: Brennan Manning, www.brennanmanning.com and *The Life Application Bible*

Practice as long as desired.

Author's Note: This simple breath is a profound practice when we remember that with each breath we are proclaiming that we did not receive a spirit of fear but the *Spirit of sonship*. We belong to our heavenly *Abba*, Father.

Mantras

Om Jesu Christaya Paramatmane Purusha Avataraya Namaha (5)

Om – universal creative sound

Jesu Christaya – Jesus Christ

Paramatmane – presiding soul of all souls

Purusha – Divine Oversoul
Avataraya – world teacher
This mantra is said in praise of Jesus. The translation reminds us that Jesus is a world teacher, *Avataraya,* and carries the authority of the Divine transcendental, *Purusha,* or God.
Repeat 108+ times.

Source: *Healing Mantras,* p.185, by Thomas Ashley-Farrand (Namadeva Acharya)

Author's Note: This mantra is a wonderful way to align with the spirit of Jesus to receive the true message in the teachings of this one called a *presiding soul of all souls.*

Sixth Beatitude: Blessed are the pure in heart: for they shall see God (1,2,3,4,5)

Tubwayhun layleyn dadkeyn b'lebhon d'hinnon nehzun l'alah
Tubwayhun: Blessed
layleyn – to those – roots go back to an image of one watching by night, waiting by lamplight for something to happen – a kind of desire that creates a vortex of possibility that draws in the object of the heart
dadkeyn – refers to those "consistent" in love or sympathy, those who have both a natural sense of influence and abundance and a fixed, electrifying purpose. The old roots call up the image of a flower blossoming because that is its nature.
B'lebhon – translated as "heart" and also carries the sense of any center from which life radiates – a sense of expansion plus generative power: vitality, desire, affection, courage and audacity all rolled into one.
d'hinnon – referring to those who are pure in heart
nehzun – translated as "see" but also points to inner vision or contemplation. The old roots evoke the image of a flash of lightning that appears suddenly in the sky: the way insight comes.
L'ahaha – God or the One. The roots point to the force and

passionate movement of the cosmos through the soul of every living thing.
Repeat as desired.

Source: Matthew 5:8, *Life Application Bible;* Aramaic translation from *Prayers of the Cosmos,* pp.62-63, by Neil Douglas-Klotz

Author's Note: This Beatitude is considered a key teaching in the Sermon on the Mount and chanting it truly quickens the heart with a remembrance that, if we can be pure of heart, we too shall see God. With commitment to our daily practice, we can cultivate *new* eyes to see, *new* ears to hear and a *new* heart to know.

Ave Maria, Gratia Plena (3,4,5)
Ave Maria – Hail Mary
Gratia Plena – Full of Grace
From Luke 1:28, *The angel went to her and said, "Greetings, you who are highly favored! The Lord is with you."* The mantra uses the words of the Angel Gabriel when he announced to Mary that she was to bear the Christ child.
Repeat as desired.

Source: *The Life Application Bible*

Author's Note: Invite yourself into the realization that, as Christian mystic Meister Eckhart said, "We are all meant to be mothers of God . . . for God is always needing to be born." This happens when we are able to fully align our will with Divine will to bring forth our unique purpose in creation.

Lord's Prayer Opening Line: Awoon dwashmaya (4,5)
Awoon – derived from *Abba* [See *Abba: I Belong to You* breath practice at the beginning of this section on Christian practices] referring to an almost childlike "daddy" or "papa" conjuring up feelings of an intimate, loving and compassionate presence. When we call God "Father" we acknowledge our kinship with Him as we would a parent.
Dwashmaya – *dwashmaya* means *who is in heaven* [in the Aramaic text the verb "is" is not present]
Repeat as desired.

Source: *Setting a Trap for God,* pp.27-39, by Rocco A. Errico

Author's Note: When the disciples of Jesus asked how they should pray, Jesus answered with reciting what was to be called The Lord's Prayer. Believed to have spoken in Aramaic, Jesus would have begun by saying *Awoon dwashmaya,* commonly interpreted from the Greek as "Our Father which art in Heaven . . ." However, translating and examining the opening phrase through the lens of the Aramaic language, new and expanded meanings are revealed. *Awoon* stirs a memory of what exists eternal beyond, yet full supporting, our daily experience. *Dwashmaya* reveals the entire manifested world as we experience through our senses or what makes the eternal aspect knowable. So, in chanting this phrase in Aramaic, we are connecting our eternal Soul with the experience of our daily human journey in the world of manifestation. We become whole.

The Lord's Prayer (1,2,3,4,5)

Translation and transliteration of the Aramaic

Bold = accent; *italics = slight guttural sound*

General Aramaic Interpretation in Italics

Aramaic Transliteration in Parentheses

Our Father which art in Heaven.	Abwoon d'bwashmaya.
Remember . . .	(Ah b**woon** deh'baush **maya**)
Hallowed be thy name.	Nethqadash shmakh.
Create Space . . .	(net **kau** dish shm*uck*)
Thy kingdom come.	Teytey malkuthakh.
Align with the Creator . . .	(taa taa **maul** koo *tah*)
Thy will be done	Nehwey sebyanach aykanna
Manifest the Vision . . .	(***ne***whay se bee **ya***na* ikana)
in earth as it is in heaven.	D'bwashmaya aph b'arha.
Become Heaven on Earth . . .	(deh'baush **maya off** bah'are **ahhhh)**

Give us this day our daily bread; ***Remember Fullness*** . . .	Hawvlan lachma d'sunqanan yaomana; (**hauv** laun **lo*ck*** mah d'soon kau nan yah oh **ma**na)
[And] Forgive our trespasses (debts) ***Forgive Self . . .***	Washboqlan khaubayn (wakhtahayn) (**wash** bah **claun** *how* **bain** *walk* tau **hain)**
as we forgive those who trespass against us. ***Forgive Others . . .***	Aykana daph khnan shbwoqa l'khayyabayn. (i**kana** *duf* **kahnan** ***shwa*** kau nal' **hi** ya bain)
[And] lead us not into temptation; ***Resist Forgetfulness . . .***	Wela tahlan l'nesyuna; (**way lah** *tau* laun **leh'**neh **su**na)
but deliver us from evil. ***Cultivate Harmony . . .***	Ela patzan min bisha. (**aa** lah patzan men **bee** sha)
For Thine is the kingdom ***For Thine is the Vision . . .***	Metol dilakhie malkutha (meh tool deh ***lahk*** hay **maul** koo *tah*)
the power, and the glory ***the Energy . . . and the Song . . .***	wahayla wateshbukhta (*wah* **hi** lah wah tesh ***book*** tah)
forever and ever. Amen ***Amen.***	l'ahlam almin. Ameyn (l'ah**laum** al**mean** ah **main**)

Repeat as desired.

Source: The Aramaic translation in the right column is from *Prayers of the Cosmos,* pp.10-41, by Neil Douglas-Klotz. (Note that Neil Douglas-Klotz's spelling of the opening line, *Abwoon d'bwashmaya,* is slightly different from Rocco A. Errico's rendering of the line in the previous practice, *Lord's Prayer Opening Line: Awoon dwashmaya.*) The transliteration in the right column as well as the general Aramaic interpretation in the left column is the author's.

Author's Note: The reader is invited to reference the author's book, *Living the Prayer of Jesus: A Study of the Lord's Prayer in Aramaic,* available on Amazon, for a complete study of the Prayer. Reciting the Lord's Prayer in Aramaic opens awareness to the inner teachings of the Prayer in ways that are difficult to articulate. For many, it has birthed a new devotion to the Prayer specifically and to the teachings of Jesus in general.

*Good resources for information are Neil Douglas-Klotz at the Abwoon Resource Center in Worthington, Ohio, www.abwoon.org, Rocco A. Errico at the Noohra Foundation, Inc., www.noohra.com, and Robert A. Jonas of the Empty Bell, www.emptybell.org.

Sufism

Note: Most Sufi lineages trace themselves back to the Prophet Mohammed, so in this way Sufism shares a common ground with Islam. However, the central idea of Sufism is believed to have existed from the beginning of creation and can be heard in the voices of all the prophets and prophetesses. As mentioned in the *Introduction: The Journey to Now: A Personal Reflection of Acknowledgment,* I had the great blessing to learn and experience the breath practices and mantras, or sacred phrases, offered here during several years of study at SAMA, the Cambridge, MA, Center of the Sufi Ruhaniat International. The Ruhaniat is a branch of Universal Sufism stemming from Hazrat Inayat Khan and Murshid Samuel Lewis.

Breath Practices

Breath of Light

On the "in" breath mentally repeat *Ya Rassoul*
On the "out" breath mentally repeat *Ya Makboul*
Ya Rassoul: Breathe in blessings of Light from the whole universe.
Ya Makboul: Breathe out the feeling of your own light being an expression of that Light.
Practice 10+ minutes.

Source: Esoteric Teachings from the Sufi Ruhaniat International

Author's Note: This is a simple and beautiful breath practice that instantly reminds us that we are made of Light yet, much like differently colored light bulbs, we each have our own unique expression of that Light.

Purification Breaths

Preferably, begin standing and proceed in a relaxed and unconstrained manner.
Inhale-Exhale through the nose 5 times
Inhale through the nose-Exhale through the mouth 5 times
Inhale through the mouth-Exhale through the nose 5 times
Inhale-Exhale through the mouth 5 times
Inhale-Exhale through the nose 5 times imagining all of your pores and cells are breathing, cleansing and healing.
Repeat as desired.

Source: Esoteric Teachings of Hazrat Inyat Khan from the Sufi Ruhaniat International

Author's Note: This is one of the few breath practices that, ideally, is practiced standing up. You will find this adds an important dimension as it teaches us to "practice relaxing where we stand."

Healing Breaths (With Sacred Phrase)

Ya Shafee – O Healer
Ya Kaffee – O Remedy
As you inhale, mentally repeat *Ya Shafee.*
As you exhale, mentally repeat *Ya Kaffee.*
Practice 10+ minutes.

Source: Esoteric Teachings from the Sufi Ruhaniat International

Author's Note: This powerful healing breath engages our mental energies to support a remembrance that the Beloved is in each breath we take as both healer and remedy. How wonderful to know that healing is only a breath away.

Sacred Phrases

*Those familiar with Islamic and Sufi practices will recognize the sacred phrases below as some of the 99 Beautiful Names of God mentioned in the Quran. I present them here, in pairs, as

I learned them in my esoteric studies with the Sufi Ruhaniat International.

Ya Ahad Ya Samad (4,5)

For this practice, it is helpful to use a visual image of a dot in the center of a circle.

Ya Ahad – "The One" (illustrated by the "dot")

The dot symbolizes the unique, mysterious you – the place in your heart that is so precious to you that you alone can feel it, sense it, embody it.

Ya Samad – "The Infinite" (illustrated by the "circle")

The circle symbolizes the infinite place of refuge that engulfs us when we fall into the heart of God, live in the heart of God and surrender to the mystery that is us.

Suggestion: Create your own image of a dot in the center of a circle. Meditate on the image as you repeat *Ya Ahad Ya Samad* 101+ times.

Source: Esoteric Teachings from the Sufi Ruhaniat International and *The Sufi Book of Life,* p.184 and p.186, by Neil Douglas-Klotz

Author's Note: When I introduce this practice, I often describe the "dot" as the embodiment of our soul's purpose and the surrounding "circle" as all the forces of the universe that are there, just waiting, to support our walk when we dare to embrace our true calling.

Ya Qadir, Ya Muqtadir (3,4,5)

Ya Qadir reminds us that everything in the universe is connected by the Divine

Strength of the One and awakens us to this unlimited Power enabling us to both manifest and contain manifestation.

Invocation of *Ya Qadir* is an antidote to feeling worthless, powerless, and to the belief that one is living a wasted life.

Ya Muqtadir is the One who places us on a particular path to God, enables us to firmly put our feet on that path, and supports us to keep going on that path, step by step, by placing one foot in front of the other. *Ya Muqtadir* brings the ability to actualize our Divine Purpose.

Repeat *Ya Qadir Ya Muqtadir* 101+ times.

Source: Source: Esoteric Teachings from the Sufi Ruhaniat International and *The Sufi Book of Life*, p.189 and p.192, by Neil Douglas-Klotz

Author's Note: This practice is wonderful for those who are in search of what their true purpose might be. It enables an inner cultivation of inner power so that personal will may be in service to divine will.

Ya Wasi Ya Wali (1,3,5)

Ya Wasi – "Limitless Expansive Capacity"
Ya Wasi invites us to expand the capacity of the heart to hold and embrace whatever may come into our orbit. Here we remember that we are never alone and that we can be present for any circumstance when our heart is fully open and expansive.
Ya Wali – "The Nearest Friend"
Ya Wali reminds us that there is no sweeter or more intimate friend than the beloved.
Repeat *Ya Wasi Ya Wali* 101+ times.

Source: Esoteric Teachings from the Sufi Ruhaniat International and *The Sufi Book of Life*, p.122 and p.150, by Neil Douglas-Klotz

Author's Note: This practice is the antidote to the core fear that we are alone. It reminds us that, no matter what may come into our experience, we can turn to our inner Beloved who is, indeed, our closest, sweetest, most intimate friend.

Ya Ra'uf Ya Rahim (1,2,3,5)

Ya Ra'uf – "Healing Love"
Ya Ra'uf specifically addresses past wounds we've received from family or humanity. It evokes a sense of resting in God in the midst of fear, hostility and struggle.
Ya Rahim – "The Moon of Love"
Ya Rahim evokes a sense of compassionate receptivity. Reciting *Ya Rahim* opens us to receive love and compassion wherever we need it most.
Repeat *Ya Ra'uf Ya Rahim* 101+ times.

Source: Esoteric Teachings from the Sufi Ruhaniat International and *The Sufi Book of Life,* p.228 and p.9, by Neil Douglas-Klotz

Author's Note: This is a deeply healing practice that I have been blessed to witness transform the most profound hurts and feelings of injustice. It makes good compost of our hurts so we may begin to imagine growing new awareness and possibilities.

Ya Ghaffar Ya Ghafour; Ya Tawwab Ya Afuw (1,2,4,5)

Ya Ghaffar calls out to Divine Forgiveness, particularly for that mistake we make
over and over again, to burn away tension and hurt.
Ya Ghafour calls out to Divine Forgiveness to penetrate to the depths of our hearts with light, particularly to that which we find unforgiveable.
**Ya Ghaffar* and *Ya Ghafour* have been described as repairing cracks in the dried out leather water carrier bringing suppleness back into our life. It is important to remember that forgiveness is a process whereby we soften our own heart to heal those places inside of ourselves where we hold hurt, anger, judgment and criticism.
Repeat *Ya Ghaffar Ya Ghafour* 101+ times.

Author's Note: I usually recommend that *Ya Ghaffar* and *Ya Ghafour* be taken on as a practice for at least forty days before adding *Ya Tawwab Ya Afuw.* This is a profound practice for forgiveness that unfolds and heals us in stages. Let's honor each stage as it is revealed allowing spaciousness for the deepest emotions to emerge. Peace is waiting at the journey's end.

Ya Tawwab – We turn away from the fault to turn to face God – and there we find God looking at us.
Ya Afuw – At this stage of forgiveness, we completely let go of the fault. The wind has completely erased the tracks in the sand.
Repeat *Ya Tawwab Ya Afuw* 101+ times.

Source: Esoteric Teachings from the Sufi Ruhaniat International and *The Sufi Book of Life,* p.39, p.92, p.221, p.226, by Neil Douglas-Klotz

*Good resources for information through the Sufi Ruhaniat International, www.ruhaniat.org, are Murshida Halima and Murshid Abraham Sussman at SAMA, www.northeastsufis.org and Murshid Neil Douglas-Klotz at www.abwoon.com.

Part 5

Extraordinary Stories from Ordinary People Using Mantra Prayer

Jan's Story

Mantra operates somewhat like salve on a tender and/or agitated mind. When our energetics are out of kilter and our minds tend to want to take our discerning thoughts hostage, mantra can offer relief.

Following participation in Reverend Rutt's *Sanskrit Mantra* course and sitting through several 40 day *Sadhanas* over the years, my mind became accustomed to resting in the energetics of certain sacred phrases. When my body gave me signs that my mind was about to run away with me, I would apply the remedy of a mantra.

Sometimes the results were startling.

At one point in her life my daughter made the clear decision to make her way to Ghana in Africa. This was made possible by her clarity and a particularly affordable flight. We pounced on the opportunity, calling the airline to secure the flight. Unfortunately, the agent said that that flight and price were no longer available. That offer was off the table. I began to feel my stomach sinking. The agent could sense this and I asked if there was another flight that my daughter might fly out on. She said she would check. I was placed on hold, my mind poised to respond in agitation to my body's disappointment and mounting anxiety.

Instead, while placed on hold for a lengthy time, I chose to focus on the possibility of another affordable flight, even if on a less than ideal travel day. To soothe my unraveling self while waiting, I used the *Ganapatayae* mantra: "to remove obstacles to your goal."

Om Gum Ganapatayae Namaha, Om Gum Ganapatayae Namaha, Om Gum Ganapatayae Namaha, etc., salutations to *Ganesha* for overcoming obstacles!

"I'm sorry, there's nothing available. Could she fly on yet another day?"

Om Gum, Gum, Gum, Gum, Gum, Gum, Gum, Gum being the seed sound for obstacle removal. I repeated this quietly to myself as the agent placed me back on hold.

"Oh!" The agent's voice burst back on the phone. She was baffled, "I don't understand how this happened but the original flight at the original price just popped back up!"

We accepted it immediately with delight – before rational thoughts might make it disappear once again!

But the story continues; complications arose around receiving the visa from New York. I was beginning to feel that the trip might not be in the cards. There was that frustrated sinking feeling again. I could feel myself beginning to rev up. Deep breath! *"Om Gum, Gum, Gum, Gum, Gum, Om Gum Ganapatayae Namaha . . . !"* I am hearing the woman say, "The visa office is closed now and the gentleman who was processing the paperwork left early for the holiday and you won't receive your travel papers in time. The office is closed on Monday. Sorry, nothing I can do!"

As I was preparing to find a way to break the news to my daughter I headed out through the garage to my car. Soon after hanging up the phone and following that emphatic, "Sorry!" I saw there placed on the steps was the package containing the visa! We still have no idea how or when it got there!

I offered my gratitude to *Ganesha*, and to the Mystery, and was able to wish my daughter "bon voyage!" She had a safe and successful trip.

Peggy's Story

I began to practice the Lord's Prayer in Aramaic in May of 2013. Having had a spiritual experience, I felt drawn to this as a necessary response to help me understand and dedicate myself to my new found life. Raised as a Catholic, I was familiar with the Lord's Prayer since the early 1960's. Yet, I was not drawn to recite it other than out of necessity during services.

After having heard the Lords' Prayer in Aramaic recited during a seminarian training class, my heart was stolen. I was captured by the beauty of it. Then I learned the more accurate translation of our Beloved's words . . . and it all became so clear to me. How the ancient words permeated my being, reaching deep into my soul, as a long forgotten primal prayer. This Prayer is with me each and every day now. I find myself calling out the words and basking in the light of our Beloved each time I do. The Aramaic Lord's Prayer reaches across the infinite life of my soul and carries me during times of weakness, and raises me above the ordinariness of my day and connects me to our Creator as no other prayer or action in my life has. I have been blessed by having this prayer as a part of my life and the experiences that have followed are, to say the least, gifts directly from our Beloved.

Cate's Story

When I first began chanting mantra, I was at the lowest point of my life. I told a friend, "I have a death wish and I need a life wish." She said, "The only thing I know to tell you to do is chant *Nam Myoho Renge Kyo*." And I did. I was instructed to chant for my happiness. My teacher said, "If you cannot believe in your happiness, or that you deserve it or even that happiness is possible, chant then for the potential for your happiness." I was also told to treat the mantra like a scientific experiment, to see if it works. To determine that, I was told to chant for something very specific - a material item, with a definite price, and all the details I cared to specify - the more the merrier. I was over 30k in debt at that time, living with two elderly parents who had to make a rapid move from their home of forty years because they'd lost their savings. I wrote and chanted and thought and doubted and chanted some more for what I wanted. Six months later, I drove a brand new cherry red Honda off the lot. I thought to my mantra, "Okay, you've got my attention."

I started to chant for everything I wanted, especially the impossible. I chanted for everyone, in the full assurance that my chanting was doing them good. I got most things for which I chanted, and when I didn't get them, I lost my wanting. My chanting became the opening to greater and greater possibilities.

When I chant mantra, I am transported by the vehicle of God. It is a fully visceral and embodied experience, with internal benefits like improved mood, patience, and hope. It's an energy raising, bliss building, peace realizing, utterly enlivening relaxation practice. The more I chant, the more devoted I am to chanting. Mantra brings gifts as the doorway to smashing skepticism. It provides me with joy and solace, humbling and making me eternally grateful. I am devoted to chanting because it makes me a vehicle, a vessel, a channel, a lamp, a ladder, a life boat for bringing the divine into our world. It affords me the means to return my blessings and joy to others.

If ever I were to choose a *Sanskrit* name, it will be Mantra.

Sharon's Story

In my thirties, I experienced panic attacks, especially while driving on the highway in heavy traffic. What kept me going and got me through was *Aad Gurey Namay,Jugaad Gurey Namay, Sat Gurey Namay, Siri Guru Deva Namay.* I would chant it over and over again until I got through whatever rough patch was there, and I still use it to this day when I feel uncomfortable about anything. Spiritual grace to all who use this chant. *Sat Nam.*

Deb-Ellen's Story

I began my practice with the chanting of *Ya Ahad, Ya Samad*. Not having any experience outside of Gregorian or *Taize* chant, I have sort of been crafting my chant from my daily experiences. In the first few months, I seemed to really be reciting these names of the Most Holy One while using prayer beads. Then, over the past four months, becoming more focused and centered, I have found myself refining my practice. I have added a very simple melody to my chant and somehow I have incorporated a process similar to leavening where I am rocking back and forth with most of my physical body in tune with my chant and vice versa. By involving more of my body, I feel not just my voice is tapping into the Universal Rhythm or Vibration but my whole being is entering into the Divine Voice or Dance. This chanting experience for me seems to both awaken me and, at the same time, draw me more deeply into a Centered Presence.

Sue's Story

Learning the 23rd Psalm in Hebrew has changed my life. I now say it every morning as part of my daily meditation. God as my Shepherd has given me a closer relationship with God. Walking through the Valley of the Shadow of Death with God has brought me comfort in difficult times. Saying the Psalm in Hebrew has opened my understanding of the passages. I feel I am closer to living God's will through making this Psalm a part of my daily life.

Bonnie's Story

I was studying the Lord's prayer in Aramaic and had been listening to the CD and reciting the words in Aramaic for a few weeks. On a day that we were to meet together for class, I was reciting the prayer for an hour while driving. Once in class, we were reciting it together when it became evident that a powerful mystical energy was present. As I looked up

I witnessed an unmistakable vision and these words began to flow from me . . .

I saw God's face in the window
It startled me
So I looked away
Rock-a-bye
I saw God's face in the window
It stirred something deep
Slowly I looked away
Rock-a-bye
I saw God's face in the window
My heart skipped a beat
I could not look away
Rock-a-bye
I saw God's face in the window
I thought it was me
And I knew I was free
Rock-a-bye
Rock-a-bye

John's Story

Eleven years ago I had coronary artery bypass surgery. Just after starting out on one of my regular runs, I noticed how quickly winded I became. Because it had happened a couple of times before, I decided to get it checked out at the emergency room. "No big deal," I told myself. Of course the ER doctor thought otherwise, wouldn't let me go home, and insisted I needed to be "transported" to the hospital, as in an "ambulance." At the hospital I flunked a stress test and an angiogram showed 80% blockage in my left main artery. Two days later I was operated on. So much for "no big deal."

People are placed in our lives for a reason. I guess I've always believed this but never took the time to reflect on it. A few years before, I found a yoga teacher named Stephanie and signed up for a class because that's what you do when you're working your way through a midlife crisis. And then I decided to take a course on spiritual development from Stephanie because I thought she was on the right path (whatever that was) and wanted some of that for myself. And then life happened, as in the coronary artery bypass, and I found myself sitting on a lawn chair during the first meeting of the spiritual development class because I couldn't yet sit on the floor after surgery. Right about then I knew it was important to be there because things stopped happening to *me* and *I started happening*. So, when I was introduced to mantras as part of the class and realized I could get to peace and healing without thinking my way there, it was a revelation. The only thing I needed was me and intention.

The mantra Stephanie gave me was *Om Ram Ramaya Swaha*, to balance healing energy channels in the body. I said it faithfully for months and still repeat it from time to time. Almost immediately I noticed its effect on bringing about a state of clarity and well-being. Later, during cardiac rehab, I noticed that I could actually bring about measurable cardiac changes in the body by repeating the mantra. My physical goal was to resume distance running and my doctor frequently told me that my artery bypass surgery should result in better performance than ever.

In cardiac rehab I ran on a treadmill with my body wired up to measure heart rate and blood pressure, the numbers displayed on a computer screen above the treadmill and a nurse carefully observing everything. I had a target heart rate range that it was important not to exceed. After a while I noticed that I could actually reduce my heart rate and blood pressure if I repeated the mantra while running. At first the nurse asked what I was saying and I would simply respond with, "It's my mantra." Later, if she noticed my heart rate was too high she would suggest I decrease the speed of the treadmill and I would tell her I could get my heart rate down with the mantra. So I began repeating *Om Ram Ramaya Swaha* and she watched the numbers on the monitors slowly work their way down. The highlight of our teamwork was when I was going for my best time ever for three miles and she yelled, "I need about two minutes of mantra."

Camilla's Story

In the second class of our first year of seminary in the Tree of Life Interfaith Seminary program at the Tree of Life School for Sacred Living, Rev. Stephanie invited us to establish a daily spiritual practice or *Sadhana.* I already meditated – fairly casually, on and off over the past 30 years or so. But Rev. Stephanie was looking for a little more commitment and structure. I was ready.

I read all the relevant pages in the *Path of Crow – Journey to Your Inner Treasure,* handbook that Rev. Stephanie had written, and I also took her up on the invitation of a one-on-one meeting to discuss what I would be doing for my daily spiritual practice. I'd decided on a 31 minute total time, as I read this brings changes to the *pranic* body, and 31 minutes felt right for me.

The structure of our daily practice was to be (1) stating our intention, (2) a breath meditation, (3) a mantra meditation, (4) traditional sitting meditation or centering prayer and (5) restating our intention. Rev. Stephanie wisely intuited and recommended for me a Sikh breath meditation for the release of subconscious fear, and she said that I could choose one of the mantras/chants from the few that she would sing to me. I hadn't ever heard any chants or mantras like these and was enjoying listening to them. Then she began to sing the mantra *Gobinday Mukanday,* and it literally brought tears to my eyes. My whole being was resonating with that mantra. I felt like she was singing to my soul.

On my way home, I went to an appointment to have our car serviced, and while waiting, I was able to download the MP3 of PREM with Snatam Kaur singing *Gobinday* onto my iPhone.

I had *Gobinday* blasting on my car speakers all the way home with the most enormous smile on my face. I felt like I was beaming with love. The whole of this rendition of *Gobinday* is only 11 minutes but I couldn't believe how soul-nourishing it felt. When I got home I was also excited to find an online "mantrapedia" at http://www.spiritvoyage.com/mantra/Aa-Oo-Um/MAN-000178.aspx where I found the words, and their meaning, and started exploring other mantras and chants as well.

> *Gobinday* – sustaining
> *Mukanday* – liberating
> *Udaaray* – enlightening
> *Apaaray* – infinite
> *Hareeung* – destroying
> *Kareeung* – creating
> *Nirnaamay* – nameless
> *Akaamay* – desireless

Rev. Stephanie opened up a whole new world of ways to nourish my soul with mantras and chants, and it's a world that I continue to enjoy exploring.

Ilona's Story

As a hospice chaplain, several times it seemed appropriate to offer to say the Lord's Prayer in Aramaic to people I visited. My experience has been that each time as I recite, they close their eyes and this sense of peace descends. The response has been "beautiful" or a simple smile. These have been moments to hold in the heart.

Linda's Story

For as long as I can remember, I have not loved myself. In fact, I actively hated myself, as was manifested in eight years of depression during my thirties. Over many years of spiritual work, including meditation, study and yoga, I was able to improve my way of being in the world, to become more present, and to be happier. However, I still did not love myself. I didn't know how to.

I came to Stephanie for other reasons – trying to find my divine path -- but quickly realized (with Stephanie's guidance) that I could not explore my divine path if I did not yet love myself. This was my major stumbling block. Stephanie gave me a mantra to recite each morning and I did it religiously. I repeated the words *"Om Gum Ganapatayae Namaha"* 108 times and thanked *Ganapati* for transforming in me whatever was preventing me from loving myself. I also found a picture of myself in college when I first became aware that I did not love myself and tried to tell this younger me that I loved her. Total blank - I would stare at my photo and not know what to say. So, I would just say that to my photo – "I don't know how to love you." I also worked on feeling what my heart felt like when I was doing this exercise. At first, it felt like a cold, dark, stone.

Slowly, over time, my heart started to thaw, warm up and open. I think this was the first sign that something was happening. Each morning – mantra, photo, heart. . . . Then, one day, after a month or so, I did the mantra, picked up the picture, looked at myself, and said "I love you." Just like that. I was shocked, but thrilled. It was so incredibly powerful . . . how doing this mantra for only several weeks had helped me undo 53 years of self-hate.

Stephanie had assured me that mantras can help undo something that has built up over years in a very short time and my experience is evidence of that. I can truly say that I love myself now and that is worth everything. I continue to use this mantra and am convinced of its power and usefulness in helping us all become more peaceful, equanimous beings.

Carol's Story

Some time ago I began a daily practice. I was given the mantra *Ardaas Bayhee*, to chant for meditation. I remember doing this for ten to fifteen days. Then one day, I heard a new mantra that I had no recollection of. I continued my practice with the mantra that I received though this new mantra continued to call to me. I did not realize it at first, but it became so strong I unconsciously began chanting it in place of my assigned practice. The name of this mantra is *Narayan Shabad*, for Purity and Peace. The translation is: 'Flawless Name is the flow of *Narayan'*. When chanting it with the tongue, all mistakes are washed away. *Narayan* gives Peace and Bliss. Following this chant is the chant *Gobina* (courage). Following this is *Sat Narayan*. I continued to chant these mantras and still chant them today. The practice has exceeded the normal forty days and lasts about an hour.

I am presently in the middle of a tremendous transformation in my life. I have sought this change and ownership of my life for more than four years. In the beginning, I had difficulty with approaching the transition, mostly because of fear; fear of failing, fear of stepping up and directly engaging my dharma. The challenge of navigating the role of my dharma with running a business was momentous. The exchange of the mantras facilitated an empowerment allowing me to confront my dharma. The mantra transformed my 'self' in that I felt stronger and believed in the 'Self'.

This revelation has strengthened my purpose and further extends my belief in the scaffold of healing and spirituality that permeates the vibrations of the mantra.

Julia's Story

I have something really *WA!* to share with you. Earlier this week, the mantra *Gayatri* called out to me like a seductive siren --only She was the one that led me safely to shore.

For a month, I'd been sailing the rocky seas of mid-winter blues and fighting a beast of a sinus infection. I heeded the siren's call and downloaded the Thomas Ashley-Farrand (Namadeva Acharya) version of this particular mantra, laughing out loud when I first heard it. "Way too fast!" I thought, "Time for the Amazing Slow Downer"--this cool software I'd recently purchased to learn some tricky choral music.

I imported the "Mother of All Mantras" and began to study it. At 50% speed, I could barely keep up with Namadeva. Slowly, over an hour's time and laughing at every turn, I sped it up. 80% speed was perfect. Looking for more (of course) I turned it up to 100%. More joy! I managed to do at least 108 repetitions during the whole session. The mantra *"Gayatri"* helped me follow an inner impulse . . . to lift myself up and out . . . and connected me to the Universe and my Beloved once more. AUMMMMMMMMMMMMMMMMM!

Stephanie's Story

I have had many experiences of Grace in my life but this is one of the most profound. I was left humbled, quieted, and deeply touched with a kind of knowing that there is just no way I could ever expand wide enough, feel deeply enough, contain fully enough . . . all the Grace that is us. I offer the following with a prayer that, within its telling, there will be something that will touch each of you in a way that will best serve your journey.

I call this story *The Mother Teresa Rosary: The Next Chapter.* It is the "Next Chapter," as the first incident occurred many years ago and is told in my first book, *An Ordinary Life Transformed: Lessons for Everyone from the Bhagavad Gita,* on pgs. 153-154.

What follows here is a simple accounting of what happened. Once in it, I started recording in my spiritual diary as I sensed I was in the midst of Grace unfolding . . .

~~~~~~~~~~~

On the morning of November 21st, 2010, half an hour before the start of a day-long seminary class, I felt a strange sensation. I went to the bathroom and saw that I was bleeding. Being 5+ years post menopausal, I instinctively knew this was not good.
~~~~~~~~~~~

After making a quick run to the store for emergency protection, I walked back into the Tree of Life and looked at my tapestry of Mother Teresa hanging on the wall. I remembered how she carried on, fully committed to her mission, regardless of what was happening within or around her. I would do the same. I and my students went on to have a great day.

That night, as I lay in bed, I rested my hands gently on my belly and felt the full weight of the morning's discovery come over me. All I could do was release as every cell in my body surrendered into my soft bed. I knew fully this was not something I was going to figure out. My only prayer was to simply rest in the sweet care of my God – the only place I knew was always totally and completely there even as all else could feel so challenging and uncertain. I had known this place. I had fallen asleep here before . . . and would likely do so again.

The next day I made an appointment with my doctor and went out for some errands. When I returned home, my husband told me there was a message on our answering machine for me from Dick, the barber. Except to wave through the barbershop window, I had not seen Dick to have a conversation in about a year and a half. My husband got his hair cut once a month so we had stayed connected that way. But, he had never called me. In the message, he said he and his wife had just returned from Chimayo and that he had brought something back for me. (Chimayo is where I had bought my first Mother Teresa Rosary many years before – a rosary that I "lost" and Dick had "found" – which he'd always believed had healed his daughter – before he was finally able to return it to me in a way neither of us could have foreseen. I tell the full story in *An Ordinary Life Transformed: Lessons for Everyone from the Bhagavad Gita.*) He asked that I stop into the barbershop sometime to pick up what he had for me. Then he said, "I love you. God bless you." Although we were certainly deeply connected because of the experience with the rosary, he had never spoken to me in that way. I remember feeling struck – that something important was happening.

It was Thanksgiving week so I knew Dick would be closed and would not open until the following Tuesday as he was always closed on Mondays. Meanwhile, I was given an appointment with my doctor for that same Tuesday. At my doctor's visit, I was told I needed to see a gynecologist for tests to rule out uterine cancer. Right after the visit, I went by the barbershop to see Dick. He was very busy but clearly glad to see me as he handed me a special Mother Teresa Rosary with hearts on it he'd brought back from Chimayo. I hugged him fiercely as he jokingly told me to take off. But, when he turned his back to me I heard clearly, "Don't worry. We've got you covered. We put you in." Chimayo is known as a place of great healing as the Mother Mary was spotted there. There are crutches on the walls, notes, etc. I knew, in that moment, I was in trouble and, also, that I was going to be ok – regardless of the outcome. And, of course, Dick could have had no way of knowing, consciously, what was going on with me.

For many years I have had a daily spiritual practice. The day after I saw the bleeding, I started a special healing practice using an ancient Vedic mantra of Shiva, the *Maha Mrityunjaya Mantra* well known for its healing properties:

Om Haum Joom Saha
Om Bhur Bhuvaha Swaha
Om Trayum-bakam Yajamahe
Sughan'dhim Pushti Vardanam
Urvaru'kamiva Bandhanan
Mrityor Mukshiya Mamritat
Swaha Bhuvaha Bhur Om
Saha Joom Haum Om

As I continued to practice the mantra, I held my new Mother Teresa Rosary against my belly and thanked her, Jesus, and the energies of Shiva for bringing ease where there was dis-ease. I fell asleep each night and awoke up each day chanting with my rosary on my belly. I started playing a beautiful instrumental of Amazing Grace constantly as I just knew some Grace was surely being played out in my life.

A few days later I had an appointment for an ultrasound. I was told by the nurse practitioner that I had a thickening of the uterine wall and a polyp. They didn't appear concerned about the polyp but said I need to return as soon as possible to see the gynecologist, to have a biopsy taken from the uterine wall. An appointment was made for the next week.

I continued on with my practice.

When I returned for the biopsy, I remembered feeling oddly calm. After the nurses prepped me, the gynecologist came in looking serious and focused. Then, as she looked more closely at the screen, I saw her whole facial expression change. She clearly looked relieved and said, "Ok, this is good. I'm happy and happy for you. When I looked at your ultrasound last week I was concerned and coming in here thought 'this is not going to be good.' But, now, your uterine wall looks thin and perfectly healthy. We should get the polyp out and we'll send it for a biopsy but it doesn't look like anything to be concerned about."

She then asked if I'd like to have it taken out before or after Christmas. Remembering that my husband would be retiring and I was uncertain as to how our medical insurance would work, I chose before. She then hesitated saying she wasn't sure she could get me in but would try. When I was sent down to the scheduling nurse, she told me she couldn't believe it but an opening had suddenly come available the following Monday morning, December 20th.

On the morning of December 20th I had the day surgery and I also shared this whole story with the special gynecologist who had served me so thoughtfully on this journey. Two days later, I received a call from her saying that all was normal.

I know I have been blessed . . . Amen

Works Cited

Part 1

Ashley-Farrand, Thomas. *The Ancient Power of Sanskrit Mantra and Ceremony,* Vol. 1, Saraswati Publications, Portland, Oregon, 2002.

Ashley-Farrand, Thomas. *Healing Mantras.* Ballantine Publishing Group, New York, New York, 1999.

Bhajan, Yogi. *The Aquarian Teacher: KRI International Kundalini Yoga Teacher Training, Level One Textbook.* Kundalini Research Institute, Santa Cruz, New Mexico, 2003.

Part 2

Ashley-Farrand, Thomas. *Healing Mantras.* Ballantine Publishing Group, New York, New York, 1999.

Tsu, Lao; Chuang-T'su. *Tao Story Man Planting Almond Tree.* Taoism – The Way – Community, www.plus.google.com/communities.

Coelho, Paulo. *The Alchemist.* HarperCollins Publishers, New York, New York, 1994.

Andrews, Andy. *The Traveler's Gift.* Thomas Nelson, Inc., Nashville, Tennessee, 2002.

Martin, Sylvia. *Origin of 'His Eye is on the Sparrow',* Wikipedia.com and Cyberhymnal.org.

Part 3

Clark, Glenn. *The Man Who Talked with the Flowers.* Macalester Park Publishing, Austin, Minnesota, 1939.

Khalsa, Shakta Kaur. *Kundalini Yoga: Unlock Your Inner Potential Through Life-Changing Exercise.* Dorling Kindersley Publishing, Inc., New York, New York, 2001.

Hurnard, Hannah. *Hinds' Feet on High Places.* Tyndale House Publishers, Inc., Wheaton, Illinois, 1975.

Satchidananda, Sri Swami. *The Living Gita: The Complete Bhagavad Gita and Commentary.* Henry Holt and Company, New York, New York, 1988.

Part 4

Ashley-Farrand. *Teacher of Mantra Instruction Manual.* Saraswati Publications, LLC., Portland, Oregon, 2007.

Ashley-Farrand, Thomas. *Healing Mantras.* Ballantine Publishing Group, New York, New York, 1999.

Kornfield, Jack. *A Path with Heart*. Bantam Books, New York, New York, 1993.

Sahn, Seung. *The Heart Sutra Commentary*. Posted by Al Jigong Billings at www.openbuddha.com., 2011.

Wildmind Buddhist Meditation, www.wildmind.org.

Khalsa, Shakta Kaur. *Kundalini Yoga: Unlock Your Inner Potential Through Life-Changing Exercise*. Dorling Kindersley Publishing, Inc., New York, New York, 2001.

Bhajan, Yogi. *The Aquarian Teacher: KRI International Kundalini Yoga Teacher Training, Level One Textbook*. Kundalini Research Institute, Santa Cruz, New Mexico, 2003.

Ginsburgh, Harav. *Gal Einai Institute*. www.inner.org.

Rosenstein, Joseph G. *Siddur Eit Ratzon*. Shiviti Publications, Highland Park, New Jerery, 2006.

Shalom Scripture Studies, Inc. www.shalom-peace.com/Psalm23.html.

Ashley-Farrand, Thomas. *Healing Mantras*. Ballantine Publishing Group, New York, New York, 1999.

Douglas-Klotz, Douglas. *Prayers of the Cosmos*. HarperCollins Publishers, New York, New York, 1994.

Errico, Rocco A. *Setting a Trap for God*. Unity House, Unity Village, Missouri, 1997.

Rutt, Stephanie. *Living the Prayer of Jesus: A Study of the Lord's Prayer in Aramaic*. Tree of Life Publishing, Amherst, New Hampshire, 2012.

Sufi Ruhaniat International. www.ruhaniat.org.

Douglas-Klotz, Douglas. *The Sufi Book of Life*. Penguin Group, New York, New York, 2005.

Part 5

Rutt, Stephanie. *An Ordinary Life Transformed: Lessons for Everyone from the Bhagavad Gita*. Hobblebush Books, Brookline, New Hampshire, 2006.

About the Author

Rev. Stephanie Rutt is an interfaith minister ordained in 2005 by the New Seminary for Interfaith Studies in New York City. She is founder of the Tree of Life Interfaith Temple and serves as Presiding Minister. She is also the founder and creator of the Tree of Life Interfaith Seminary and the Tree of Life School for Sacred Living, LLC, formally the Tree of Life Yoga Studio. In addition to having taught Kripalu and Kundalini yoga for many years, Rev. Rutt is the creator of numerous spiritual study programs including *Rise Up! The Bhagavad Gita: Job Description for a Spiritual Warrior, Living Our Purpose: The Heart of Spiritual Practice, The Lord's Prayer and Beatitudes in Aramaic,* the *Sanskrit Mantra Course* and *Kosi R'Vaya: A Study of Psalm 23*. She is the author of *An Ordinary Life Transformed: Lessons for Everyone from the Bhagavad Gita*, published by Hobblebush Books in 2006 and creator of *The Path of Crow: Journey to Your Inner Treasure*, curriculum for the Tree of Life Interfaith Seminary, and the *Spiritual Mentoring Certificate Program*. In addition, in 2012, Rev. Rutt released *The Interfaith Worship Manual* and *Living the Prayer of Jesus: A Study of the Lord's Prayer in Aramaic* through Tree of Life Publishing. Rev. Rutt is a member of *A World Alliance of Interfaith Clergy*, the *Interfaith Alliance* and the *North American Interfaith Network (NAIN)*.

As a way of extending service to the community at large, Rev. Rutt founded the Gifts of Grace Foundation which created quilts for local foster care children from 2005 through 2009 and she served as Convener of the Souhegan Valley Interfaith Council from 2004 through 2006 during which she sponsored the *To Hear How Others Pray* series.

Rev. Rutt holds a Master of Arts in Psychology, Guidance and Counseling and in the early 90s worked as a mental health counselor at Milford Regional Counseling Services and taught for many years in the behavioral science at the University of New Hampshire at Manchester. Today, she is pursuing a D.Min degree from Andover Newton Theological School.

Made in the USA
Columbia, SC
14 May 2018